Praise for **MORNING MEETING, AFT**

"*Morning Meeting, Afternoon Wrap-Up* is a book that I have provided to teachers at many professional development workshops. The book provides a structured approach to setting up a classroom for optimal learning and collaboration. The NEW edition has kept the tried and true while adding more of the tips and strategies that Donna is so famous for providing. This book is an invaluable resource for new and seasoned teachers." —*Susan Sarfaty, Regional Superintendent, St. Clair County, IL*

"When I started teaching first grade eight years ago, I had no idea how to set up a classroom, especially one that would emphasize community and trust. I bought several books that I hoped would provide guidance, but realized I had struck gold as soon as I started reading *Morning Meeting, Afternoon Wrap-Up*. Mrs. Whyte's book showed me how to structure the environment in my classroom and motivate my students in a way I hadn't realized was possible. Without a doubt, my class was the best behaved and most self-reliant group in our grade level, and all of my students felt as though they were part of a cohesive team. I only taught first grade for one year, but now, eight years later, I am about to do it again. The first thing I did was pull out my copy of *Morning Meeting, Afternoon Wrap-Up*. Not many educational books can stand the test of time, but this one is just as relevant today as it was almost a decade ago. It was a lifesaver then, and I have no doubt it will be a lifesaver again now."
—*Jennifer Brown, Classroom Teacher, Little Valley Elementary School, St. George, Utah*

"I have taught both Pre-K and Kindergarten and have found myself searching for a fun way to motivate, engage, and help keep my students focused throughout the day. *Morning Meeting, Afternoon Wrap-Up* was my answer!"
—*Georgia Matthei, Classroom Teacher, St. Patrick School, Owego, NY*

"When I changed grade levels, I knew I needed some help setting up a new classroom. The numerous ideas in *Morning Meeting, Afternoon Wrap-Up* were not only practical, but easy to implement!"
—*Connie Boggs, Classroom Teacher, Monongah Elementary School, Monongah, WV*

Donna Whyte

MORNING MEETING, AFTERNOON WRAP-UP

2nd edition

**Practical Routines to Build Community,
Motivate Learners, and Meet Standards**

Staff Development *for* EDUCATORS

Peterborough, New Hampshire

Published by SDE Professional Development Resources

10 Sharon Road, PO Box 500

Peterborough, NH 03458

1-800-321-0401

www.SDE.com/crystalsprings

Author's Note: The incidents that are used as examples in this book are real. The names of the children are not. I've changed the names, and occasionally combined separate incidents, to protect the privacy of the children in my classes.

Library of Congress Cataloging-in-Publication Data

Whyte, Donna, 1962-

  Morning meeting, afternoon wrap-up, 2nd edition : practical routines to build community, motivate learners, and meet standards / Donna Whyte. -- Second edition.

    pages cm

  ISBN 978-1-63133-020-9

  1. Classroom environment--United States. 2. Motivation in education--United States. 3. Effective teaching--United States. I. Title.

  LB3013.W49 2015

  370.15'4--dc23

                    2014029294

  Printed in the United States of America

  18 17 16 15 14   1 2 3 4 5

Dedication

This book is dedicated to the
late Joseph Tourville, and to all the other
teachers who may never truly know
what they mean to their students.

Table of Contents

Acknowledgements

I would like to thank Staff Development for Educators for the many opportunities they have provided that allow me to share my work with so many educators. Their staff development opportunities for teachers are the finest available and serve to support teachers around the globe in the important job of teaching our children.

To all the children who have help me to become a better teacher, I say, "thank you". Listening and responding to their needs has allowed me to write books and develop activities to support teachers. Each child carries a story and I am so fortunate that I have had the opportunity to be a part of so many stories.

Thank you to my husband, Mark, who believes in me and my work 110%. He is my coach, computer wizard, assistant, travel companion and the best listener in the world. He is also one of the only people that can get me to stay still long enough to complete a project. At times he has had to play the role of mom and dad, as I pursued my dream of sharing my passion for teaching and children with others. I feel so lucky to have met him over 30 years ago and that he is my life partner. He is truly the wind beneath my wings.

And a gigantic thank you to my children, Carter and Taylor. They have shared their mom with so many people over the years, always with great understanding for the profession I chose. They are the greatest joys of my life and I am blessed to be their mother.

PREFACE

The first edition of *Morning Meeting, Afternoon Wrap-Up* was published in 2004. Wow! I never dreamed it would be so popular as to last through a decade of changes in education. As teachers, we must constantly incorporate new mandates, new "hot" topics, and many new thoughts on how to effectively reach individual children in a classroom built to accommodate a group. But I believe that the ideas and strategies presented in *Morning Meeting, Afternoon Wrap-Up* have stood the test of time because they *were* and *are* all about creating a classroom in which children learn as individuals. In some ways, I think the book was ahead of its time. My first version placed great emphasis on communication, collaboration, and community-building. These concepts are now recognized as key 21st century skills! All I knew back then was that these routines helped me to create an environment where children learned at a higher level, while they accepted more responsibility for their own learning.

In the past decade, I have had many more chances to witness firsthand what works and what doesn't as we educate our youth. And so, *Morning Meeting, Afternoon Wrap-Up* deserves an update that will inspire even more teachers to create a classroom framework that encourages successful learning.

Over the years, many teachers have approached me at staff development events carrying a tattered copy of my book. They share how they built their own classroom success story using some of the ideas from the book. This updated version is for all of you. In it, you will find many new additions and ideas to support you and your students. Here's to another 10-plus years of doing the right thing for children and for their learning.

PART 1

INTRODUCTION

Where It All Began

One of the most important foundations of good teaching is establishing a strong "learning environment" in your classroom. This is a classroom where children are active participants in their own learning and where they feel that they belong—a place where children are responsible, caring, and love to learn.

I've taught and observed for years now, and what I've seen and experienced has convinced me that the classrooms where children feel most empowered in their learning are the ones where teachers teach much more than just the facts. They teach problem-solving, collaboration, and communication—skills so critical to today's world it's hard to imagine a successful person without them. They focus on helping children "learn to learn" and allowing each child to learn at his own pace.

Many of these teachers structure their day with the student-centered routines of a morning meeting and an afternoon wrap-up. What each looks like may differ, along with the goals that each of us sets for our routines. This book is my effort to share some of my own goals, experiences, and reflections with you. As you read, look for the stars to find key ideas and the suns to highlight helpful tips and activities. Here we go!

Have You Been There?

Take a look at your classroom. What does it look like when the children come in? They all have a story to share, something to show or to tell you about. Many are excited and wound like tops. You know you have a lot to do; you have to get busy to be able to fit it all in. We are telling them to unpack, get their supplies, and settle in so that we can all get started on the day. They are wondering what the day will bring, talking to peers, talking to you at the same time, and not looking very organized. We all have an agenda, and they have an agenda, too. Sometimes, it just seems that ours doesn't matter. We're asking, "Do you have a pencil, where's your journal, and are you ready to start?" and telling them to get their coats off, hand in their book slips, and put up their backpacks. These poor children are overwhelmed before we even begin the day!

The other end of the day can be so much worse. Do you see any of yourself in this? You are running ragged, realizing how much you didn't get to, and yelling, "Come on boys and girls—focus—we just have one more thing to get to." Then you realize—oh no!—The buses are here! Time has slipped away, and so much is not finished. You might sound a bit like this, "Let's go boys and girls—get packed, don't forget your books, clean up the floor, and put on your coats while you run to the bus!" You are exhausted, and everything is in fast forward now. They are gone; you look around and see the remnants of a busy day that had no closure. The room is a disaster; books that were supposed to go home are still on some of the desks, and several coats still hang in the cubbies. It feels like you ran them in, ran them out, and never finished what you started.

We've all lived there. It is not good for you, and it is not good for children. I decided that I needed to create a framework that allowed us to begin together and end together and organize our day in a way that was more conducive to learning. ★ **I wanted to build a framework that would allow us to start and end the day in a way that established and reinforced the strong, supportive environment that my children both needed and deserved.** That framework became the routines of morning meeting and afternoon wrap-up.

It's About Time

Everywhere I go, teachers tell me that the number one challenge they face in classrooms each day is that they don't have enough time. I agree. We don't *have* enough time. But sometimes the use of the time we have is not optimal for learning. We all must decide how learning happens and adjust our schedules to reflect what we know is best for children. Some teachers tell me they think that implementing the routines in *Morning Meeting, Afternoon Wrap-Up* would take up too much teaching time. I believe it is time we can't afford *not* to spend. My goal for you is to establish a framework that not only gives you more teaching time, but better quality time.

I want you to have a time when you can introduce a concept to children and quickly assess where the children are in their level of learning. Allowing for collaboration and communication among the students will often identify which child is struggling and which has an understanding of the concept that we are addressing. If a child is already answering all of the questions about the lesson correctly, then that child should not have to practice a concept in group or individual time that he has already mastered. This is a time when you make those quick adjustments for where the children are in their learning. There are days when I release children from the morning meeting to go off to do individual tasks at their level, thus enabling me to give more attention to the children who remain when I'm introducing or guiding practice of a new concept. This flexibility within the structure is imperative to gaining time and getting the most out of the time we have.

These morning and afternoon meetings will also be the times when we build community. In our battle for time, Ruth Charney wrote, "We need to remember that academics and social behavior are profoundly intertwined." Time to teach can determine both the success or failure of our classroom. ⭐ **Facilitating better learning requires building community.** And building community means building social skills—life skills that enable us to learn at higher levels.

PART 2

THE CONTEXT

Morning Meeting and Afternoon Wrap-Up, the routines with which you begin and end your day, offer a lot more than simply structure. Before we start setting up the framework, I'd like to spend a little time looking at the context in which these routines resonate so powerfully.

The Curriculum

Standards Focus

There will always be standards in education that address what each of us must teach in a given time period. While these may seem overwhelming at times, I have found that holding meetings allows me to evaluate, condense, and sometimes even skip a standard. How? I can do that by identifying what it is that my students already know and what they still need to learn. If I am introducing a standard during the meeting and realize that most of my students have mastered that standard already, then I can move that instruction into small-group time for the students who need it and use my whole-group time to move on in the curriculum.

Test this by creating a list of several standards that span grade levels and keeping the list with you at

> **Keep a list of key standards. Note which children show proficiency and who will need additional support.**

meeting time. Check off things that most students show proficiency with, and take note of the children who will need additional support. Incorporate a basic standard that crosses grade levels, such as *students will identify fiction vs nonfiction text*, and address this during a couple of meetings. Identify the children who can quickly and easily explain or identify the differences, and note that when most students can achieve the standard, it should no longer be a whole-group lesson. Check them off and begin to see the numbers of standards become more manageable.

Of course, in addition to the many academic skills we address every day, ⭐ **21st century standards ask each of us to incorporate communication, collaboration, and critical-thinking tasks into our lessons.** Meetings make this easy. Children are actively engaged in these skills each meeting, and you will be amazed at the level of communication, collaboration, and higher-level thinking that can be achieved.

Integrated Literacy

At times, you will find that you address many of the standards on your list as you do shared reading and writing activities with the group. When we take the time to show how reading, writing, listening, speaking, and viewing are interwoven, we set a stage for higher literacy competencies. Children need direct instruction and daily practice in all five components, and we can establish opportunities for all five components each day if we do shared writing in our morning meeting. We might begin by viewing an interesting image, perhaps a colorful photograph. We can discuss with the children what should be included in the writing and how it should be organized, write together, and then read through our writing and decide how to make it better.

⭐ **Each component—reading, writing, listening, speaking, and viewing—is given context and practiced via this simple shared writing as we begin the day.** If the writing is related to a science or social studies topic, we have the ability to incorporate subject matter with basic literacy. We want to introduce and reintroduce concepts to children in our morning meeting, offer guided practice, and then reflect back in our afternoon wrap-up to see how we did when we practiced independently.

Assessment

Meetings provide opportunity for daily assessment within the whole group to determine what each child needs. The benefit is that you are then able to adapt your teaching right away. Although we often lack the time for summative assessments on a daily basis, in reality, it is the simpler formative assessments that are more valuable because they allow us to be more effective in our teaching. Using formative assessment strategies to drive further instruction during the day or on the very next school day makes a huge difference for ensuring success. ⭐ **Informal assessments can be done easily within a meeting.** Asking questions that require a "thumbs-up or thumbs-down" reply can show you quickly which students are with you. If partners have small whiteboards or paddles and hold up their thinking and answers for you to view, there is an opportunity to quickly observe where they are in their understanding. At times, you might ask children to respond by using four corners of the classroom. In this informal assessment, you give a choice of four responses to a question, and each child moves to a corner of the room based on her thinking. This is another quick way to see where your students are in their learning, and it has the added benefit of getting everyone up and moving.

> **Questions that require a thumbs-up or thumbs-down response are a quick way to check which students are with you.**

Reflection

It is important that we reflect on our day by asking children what we did and why we did it. They have to make the connection explicit. Nothing is more upsetting than to hear a parent at dismissal time ask her child, "What did you do today?" and to hear a child reply, "Nothing." There are times when I am so enlightened by the answers that I receive when I ask children what we did and why. After a day in which we had several word centers set up, I asked the children why we do so many word work activities. I wanted to hear them say that working with words makes you a better reader, a better writer, and a better communicator, but instead the children replied with things like, "So we keep busy," "We learn to put activities back in the right place," and, "Because you told us to." **If we want children to be invested in their learning, they must know why they do what they do.** Meetings give you an opportunity to find out if they truly do know.

The Community

Group Effort

Wong and Wong, authors of *The First 30 Days of School*, remind us that "It is the procedures that set the class up for success to take place." It takes routines to build our community and ensure that our children learn to work together. It takes strategies and activities that outline for children how to communicate effectively with others. Over 60 years ago, Abraham Maslow presented a "Hierarchy of Needs." He wrote about building a sense of community to foster "group effort" that encourages learning. And so to foster our group effort, I need to encourage collaboration and communication among students. Get the learners more involved in their learning; create a foundation that begins and ends our learning day!

How many of you believe that you work harder than the children do? ⭐ **The truth is the one who *works* is the one who *learns*.** We need our children doing more and taking responsibility for their learning. I can't be the only teacher in the classroom. There are too many of them and only one of me. I learn so much from listening to children, and they can learn a great deal by listening and talking with each other.

Group Identity

I call the children in my class my "Smarties." I started calling them that because I wanted to name them something that they identified with. ⭐ **It's not *my* classroom. I get to come here every day only because 20-some of them join me. This is our room. Our community.** The sign on the door says, "Smarties Community, facilitated by Mrs. Whyte." It says this because that's my role inside—

facilitator. I want to build a community where children belong. That's at the heart of good teaching and getting children to learn.

In my workshops, I often ask teachers to come up with names for their classes. The teachers make up names, like "Mrs. Green's Googles." I had a teacher who said she called her children "Mrs. Fulton's Flyers" because she'd tell them, "You're flying today!"

One teacher came up with "Cupcakes." One of the other teachers was a third-grade teacher, and she said sarcastically, "Yeah, I can see me calling mine my cupcakes!" So I said, "What did you come up with?" She said, "I'll call them my dudes—'Mrs. Denning's Dudes.'" And they probably loved that in third grade. You need to find what's comfortable for your children. You might even make a game of it: hold a little classroom survey, throw out some names and let them vote, or let them brainstorm and then vote. They take on their own identity.

Everyone Is Involved

Do we really want to choose only one of those waving hands that say, "Please, please pick me to be involved in my learning," or do we want everyone in the class involved? I think you'll agree that it is time that every child gets involved.

> Involve the group in solving any problem that impedes their ability to function and learn.

As educators, we are all aware of the importance of teaching our children to think, although I am not sure that we always follow through on this goal. We tend to "feed" children information and then ask them to give it back in the same form. True learning requires that children learn to process the information in different ways and present their thoughts. In many whole-class discussions, one child speaks at a time. At meeting times, however, we want partners and groups to learn to share so that more children are involved. Watching children wave their arms and grunt in an effort to be called on by the teacher just breaks my heart. ⭐ **Hand-waving is a signal that children want to be involved. Shouldn't we involve as many students as possible in their own learning?** The goal should be that every child is involved at a deeper level than just listening to *one* classmate. We all know that when one child is talking, most of the others are unengaged, not listening, chatting, or just wondering why they don't get called on. Let's set a goal to get all of our children involved in the learning.

Teachers often relate to me that they address a single issue *over and over* in a day. I tell them that they should bring that issue to meeting time and address it once. If there is a problem that impedes the group's ability to function and learn, then it involves *all of us*. I would present the issue and ask the children to brainstorm ideas for how to fix the problem. I would then ask them to talk to their partners about the benefits and drawbacks of their solutions. This is problem-solving, communication, and collaboration at its finest.

An Illinois teacher who attended one of my workshops listened to this idea and said that she thought there was a slim chance that her children would be able to discuss and solve a problem without her input. So, she decided to try it. She wrote to me later to say she was shocked about the level of commitment to the solution when it was her students' idea.

Many teachers tell me that they have a hard time letting go of some of the control. But they also realize that for students to reap the benefits when they learn to think at a higher level and to commit more strongly, everyone must be involved in the process.

Do the Right Thing

The rules of meeting time are no different from the rules enforced the rest of our day. You will need to decide how you set up the rules in your classroom. I am a believer that I only need to establish one rule that can encompass all of what we need to do to be successful in the classroom and in life. That rule is "Do the Right Thing." I have never assumed that the children know what I mean by the right thing, so I conduct mini-lessons in our meetings at the beginning of the year to exemplify what the right thing looks like, sounds like, and even feels like. This teaches the children what's expected of them and sets up the classroom for success. A sample mini-lesson gathered the children in pairs and asked partners to brainstorm and share ideas about what are the right and wrong things for you to do if someone trips near you? This is an ongoing issue in schools, and it can be addressed proactively by asking children to come up with the two lists and then holding them responsible for following through on the *right* things to do.

Fair or Equal?

Equal is everyone getting the same thing. Fair is everyone getting what they need to be successful. ★ **Meetings, along with many other parts of our day, need to acknowledge that different children need different things.** None of this is a secret to the children. They will gladly report to you who talks too much, which child is a "wiggle worm," or which student never does her work. It is NOT a secret; they all know that there are differences. I am asking each of us to acknowledge the differences and get on with the learning.

When a child is unable to sit for a period of time (such as meeting time), I say out loud, "Boys and girls, we know that Arness has a hard time sitting still, so Arness and his partner are going to stay at their seats and listen from there today; we are all coming over to our area." State it as a fact; don't leave room for discussion; and don't make a big deal out of it. Children, and sometimes teachers, will say, "That's not fair." But it is. It's fair; it's not equal. Know the difference and use it to your benefit when working with a classroom where diversity is the rule.

And here is some food for thought: Is there research that shows that sitting still with your legs crossed in a square or on a piece of tape is the best way to learn? We need to keep in mind that much of what we do in the classroom is based on what school has "always looked like," but that doesn't necessarily mean that it is the best way for children to learn. The reality is that schools are adapting every day to the learner and are not nearly as dependent on "what a classroom used to look like" as once was the case.

The Children

"You Don't Know the Child I Have!"

Teachers often share that my ideas sound great, but that I don't know the trying child or children in their class. Actually I do! I *was* that child. I was constantly out of my seat, talking, not paying attention, and not following directions. I was a nightmare for most of my teachers over the years. There are students who struggle academically, socially, or behaviorally. Some struggle with all three! The truth is that many of these children can flourish in an atmosphere where they are given opportunities to learn and practice the skills that they lack, where models for both appropriate and inappropriate behavior are demonstrated and discussed. We often punish inappropriate behavior without realizing that we have not taught a replacement behavior; therefore, when a child is put in the same position, she will revert back to the same behavior that got her in trouble in the first place.

⭐ **Meetings allow time to discuss and practice appropriate behaviors.** We also look at what the inappropriate behavior looks like, therefore eliminating any question of what it is that we expect. It is our job to assess the need and teach to it. This book is dedicated to a teacher who changed my life. Mr. Joseph Tourville was a teacher who knew what I needed to be successful. He didn't try to control me; he taught me to control myself. He would ask me how I thought I could solve the issues that arose; he would then ask if I thought my solution was a doable plan and one that I could commit to. He allowed me to model "the correct and incorrect way," giving me attention and also showing that I was capable of doing the right thing. He involved me in the process and thus created commitment on my part. We have to involve the children in all aspects of learning. ⭐ **Meetings allow us to turn the power over to the people who can make the changes.** I can't change a child, but I can create an atmosphere that allows my children to make those changes themselves.

Building Problem Solvers

We hear a great deal about the fact that our job is to create higher-level thinkers. Often we begin with low-level thinkers, and I fear that these days we have some children who do not think at all. It is so easy for our students to wait for someone else to do things for them, to get someone else to do the thinking, or to let someone else answer the questions. So I use a "rubber ball approach"—bounce the problem back to them and see if they can figure it out.

If a child states, "I don't have a pencil," I reply, "What do you do if you don't have a pencil?" "Have you seen my journal?"—I say, "I don't have your journal, hon. Maybe you can look for it and think about where you might have left it."

"She said that . . . Amy said that . . . Cody said that Alejandro doesn't like me." I say, "Wow, Let's see. I didn't hear my name in there, so I must not be involved. What are you going to do?"

> **Use the rubber ball approach to bounce children's questions back and encourage them to solve their own problems.**

We must stop solving their problems for them. We spend too much of our day in charge of everyone and not creating problem-solvers or higher-level thinkers. Encourage children to think for themselves, and ask them the questions back to see if they are, in fact, doing the thinking. If they never learn to solve the little problems or answer the small questions for themselves, how will they learn to deal with the big issues or answer the harder questions? It is so important to acknowledge that the reason many of us get very tired of hearing our name called is that we have created the situation in which children feel we have all the answers. We can change that and, in the process, teach our children to think for themselves. This simple technique can become a backbone to building your community. The children will depend much more on one another when they know that you won't get involved or give them the answers.

The Student Teacher

One year it dawned on me that I spent much too much of my valuable classroom time assigning jobs, looking for the child who was in charge of a job, and keeping track of which child had had a turn doing a job. I always wished for a student teacher to come from the college to give me "extra hands," and then I realized there are lots of extra hands in my classroom. ⭐ **The mistake I was making was not using all of my students as teachers.** I decided that I would set up an exciting program for a *student teacher*—a student who did all of the jobs. We all know that enthusiasm is contagious, and the more excited I was as I outlined the job description for the students, the more excited they were to participate. They quickly forgot about all those little jobs like turn out the lights, when I described in detail how lucky each would be when it was their turn to be the student teacher. In kindergarten, I would have two student teachers (I didn't want one getting lost alone in the hallway when he had to do errands). In first, second, and third grade, there was just one student teacher. This student had a small desk next to mine for the day. It was well-equipped with teacher gadgets—tape, stapler, can of writing instruments, etc.

> Set up a student teacher program, using your own students as helpers.

The child was in charge of all the jobs and could pick a random student to help, if needed. Each day the student teacher changed; I kept track of whose turn it was by moving a clothespin down a chart of names. No worries if a student missed her day. We would skip the name, put on a different-colored clothespin, and come back to her whenever she returned to class.

With older students, you might consider allowing the student teacher to become the message writer. The children love doing this. They see it as a special privilege. You don't even have to give them any direction. You'll be surprised when you see them model what you've been doing all along. Sometimes it can be pretty funny when they start imitating you! But often the student teacher will get to the chart even before you get there.

Having jobs for everyone to do was something I had done for so long that I had never thought about how much time it took up. Children love when it is their turn to be student teacher, and I love not having to ask, "Who is in charge of . . .?" It has truly made such a large difference in how the classroom operates. It also creates responsibility beyond what having one job did in the past.

> **Include a chart in your meeting space and use it to share content with your students.**

The Meeting Area

I like to have a special area where we can meet as a group. That doesn't mean that you need to have an area that can accommodate every child in the class sitting one way. Don't worry if everyone doesn't fit on the floor in a given area. Be flexible in how children sit and where. Have a space that is conducive to meeting as a group, even if that involves some staying at a table or desk that is close to where some of the students are sitting on the floor. Some of mine sit on crates; some are on the floor; and some are on their knees in the back row. I even have one who likes to stand to the side. I allow the differences because it teaches us about true community, understanding that we all need different things. ⭐ **As long as a student is close enough to his partner to collaborate, I am pretty lenient on how he decides to get comfortable.**

I worked in a classroom where the teacher told me she wanted a place to meet but had absolutely no space. I asked her if I could offer "fresh eyes" in her room and perhaps find space. She said, "Absolutely—please try!" I immediately noted a cart in the corner with a broken TV that could be sent to storage, and a bookcase that easily could be turned to come off the wall to become a divider that took less space. With a few small adjustments, we had created a meeting area. It's sometimes hard to see differently that which you look at every day. It may help to ask someone you trust to use her "fresh eyes" to make a recommendation that could work for you.

In your meeting space, include a chart or some kind of visual display that you can use to share content with students. Place it where the children can see it. For many of you, interactive whiteboards have been placed in less than convenient areas of your rooms, so just use a chart stand if you need to. Have a crate with any supplies that you use on a regular basis for meeting time, which might include your signal bell, pointers, or talking sticks. Remember that preparation saves time, so create an area that suits your needs as well as the children's. You need a classroom set up that best uses the space you have for learning. Never sacrifice space that could be used for children in order to keep "stuff." ⭐ **Classrooms were built for students, not stuff.** I try hard to find other areas for the stuff, so that the children become the focus of how to best make use of space within the room.

And Finally

A Word of Caution

Routine is good, but it can also become just a routine! As educators, many of us know the importance of building routines with children. Many of our children do not have set routines within their homes and are often lost in terms of staying focused on tasks that drive learning. On the other hand, we know that routines can become so embedded that the students become parrots and not true learners. They just give back what they are accustomed to doing over and over. That is why it is so important to vary your activities within the meeting times. We need to challenge students' minds and get them participating, not just being passive group members. The goal is to get everyone involved. We will all learn at a higher level when we discuss, participate, and challenge our own thinking.

> **Challenge your students and get them involved by varying your meeting activities.**

A Flexible Framework

The framework needs to be flexible in order to fit the learners on any given day or time. I want there to be a beginning and an ending to our day, but I also want to acknowledge that no two days are the same. Learners also come in all shapes, sizes, and attention spans! We can create routines that allow for differences. It is good to know what to expect, but we also need to recognize that through differentiation, we will each get what we need.

We start together and end together to cement our community and our learning. Starting as a group will allow us to look forward and prepare for our day, and ending together will allow us to reflect on what we did and why it was important. It also allows us to see how our learning relates to our life outside of school.

Routine—yes! Flexibility within the routine—a must!

PART 3

MORNING MEETING

The Right Start!

Think about how you typically begin the day with the children in your classroom. Do you greet them at the door as they come in? If you do, good for you! ⭐ **I think it's important to greet children at the door in the morning.** It lets them know that you were expecting them, and you're eager to see them. Treat them as if they were guests in your home. Would you ever say, "Hey, I'm in the closet getting something. I'll be right out!" Maybe you'd do that once in a blue moon, but certainly you wouldn't do it on an ongoing basis. I want to be there at the door. I want to greet the children. I want them to know that I am waiting for them, and I want to establish a routine. It's fun to come up with different ways to greet the children. We make up funny rhymes, such as, "Come on in, Mr. Fin," and they have to swim by, or, "Welcome to the day, let's hear a neigh," and they neigh like a horse. Be on the lookout for fun ways to say good-bye in afternoon wrap-up, too.

What Can You Tell from a Face?

When the children come in in the morning, you need to pay attention to their faces. A face can tell you a lot about what kind of day that child is having. I could take one look at Jose's face and realize he was having problems. Maybe he'd gotten in trouble on the bus that morning. Then he'd lost his coat in the bus room. The cafeteria had his favorite, French toast sticks, at breakfast, but they had run out before he'd gotten there. This child was already a wreck when he arrived to class.

You have to be sure to recognize that. You have to ask what happened and then say something like, "Jose, you've gotten off to a bad start. You have a couple of choices. You can continue the way you're going. Or I can help you change some things. We can't change what happened on the bus, but I can help you look for your coat. At lunchtime, we can go down and look for your coat in the bus room, or we'll look in the lost and found. I can't make French toast sticks for you, but instead of what they had in the cafeteria, would you like a granola bar?" ⭐ **If a child is upset, give him a chance to share what's wrong. Show him his choices, and help him move on.** Otherwise, that child won't learn a thing all day because he'll still be stewing about those French toast sticks!

The Home-School Folder

For me, an important part of the morning routine is the home-school folder. It's the first thing the children bring to me in the morning and the last thing that goes out at night. At the beginning of the year, everybody receives a home-school folder that they're going to be bringing back and forth each day. Vinyl folders that won't rip are best. Ask for or buy two-pocket vinyl folders with a strip of brads down the middle. This folder is going to connect our classroom with the student's home. Anything the child's parents want me to see can be placed inside. Anything I want them to see will be placed in it at the end of the school day. It is important that your best attempt is made to connect with every child's family; therefore, it is best to create a system that enables you to keep track of families who participate and those who don't.

> **Make a daily connection between school and home with home-school folders. Give each child the same color folder. If that folder is lost, use a second color, and a third if necessary. This helps you track who is responsible and who needs help.**

Here's an easy way to keep track. At the beginning of the year, get a number of folders—enough so you have one for every child in your class, plus any new students. Make sure that each of those folders is the same color. Then, get about six to nine folders of a second color and four or five folders of a third color.

At the beginning of the year, give every child the same color folder. If the first folder is lost, use the second color. Each time that folder is returned, remind the student to take good care of it because it is their second one. If the folder were to be lost again, give the third color and be sure to reiterate how important it is that this folder travel back and forth and not be lost. The color allows you to immediately identify who is responsible with their folder and who is not. This gives you the opportunity to aid the children who need assistance with organization and responsibility without involving everyone else.

Teachers often ask me, "What if a child is on the last color within the first couple of weeks of school?" My answer is that each of us must evaluate what is best for the children we are charged with teaching. If you have tried to instill responsibility and a connection to home, you have done your job. Don't beat a dead horse. Reflect and ask yourself if this student is capable of handling the responsibility and has a home life that wants to be connected. If you answer, "Yes," then try again. If not, let it go. You can't make his parents/guardians want the connection; you can only offer the opportunity. And please never punish a child for not bringing the folder. While I stress the importance of the folder, a punishment would be a horrendous way to start a child's school day.

⭐ **Send home a letter at the beginning of the year describing the home-school folder. Tell the parents, "This is *your* connection to me. This is *my* connection to you."** Let them know how important it is to have the folder go back and forth each day. Remind them that you will look at it first thing in the morning and that they should take the opportunity to check it each afternoon. Describe how you will be using the folder this year and all that may be in it.

I provide each child with a folder. It says "Home-School Folder" right on it, so that there's no "Well, I'm using *this* folder." A simple way to label them is to use computer labels. I import the children's pictures and then make little labels that say, "I belong to Connor (or Taylor or Anise or Amanda)." Every label has a child's name and picture on it. The children love labels with their own pictures on them. And that way they can recognize their own folders even before they can read their names. This also enables students to hand out the folders before they know each other's names. They just look at the picture and give the folder to the person who looks just like it.

I use a folder with two pockets; it helps teach the concept of left and right. The left side is marked "Left at Home," so if something is in here, the student should leave it at home. The right side is "Bring Right Back," meaning that they would need to bring these papers back to you when they come to class. Remind children that if they take a paper out of the right side and it is something that needs to be signed, then they need to put it back in so that it comes back to school. But if they're taking home today's research question to show their family, that goes on the left side because they're supposed to leave it at home.

> Use a folder with two pockets; it helps teach the concept of left and right. Label each folder with the child's name and picture; this makes it easy for them to pass out folders even before they know each other's names.

You could tape resealable plastic bags inside these folders with packing or duct tape, or if you get the folders with the brad fasteners in the middle, put a pencil case with the three rings prepunched into the center of the folder. I find that if a child's going to bring lunch money, and it's an odd amount, or any other kind of little stuff, it's good if the parent can toss it into the bag or case so it doesn't get lost on the way to school. Also, use it if there is anything small to go home.

If you're a child in my class, you can count on me being at the door when you get to class each morning. You come up to me with your home-school folder in your hand; this signals the beginning of our connection. You hand your folder to me. I look you in the eye and greet you. I have a little desk next to me, and as I pull certain things out of the folder, I might say, "Oh, lunch money, good; permission slip signed, good. Thanks, hon. Good morning. Next." If somebody has a note from a parent, I see it right away because it's in the home-school folder.

Go straight down the line. Every child who comes in has to hand over her home-school folder. Before I take attendance, it's easy for me to do a quick assessment and say, "I'm missing three folders. So either three children are absent today, or somebody got by without giving me a folder." I keep the folders at my desk during the day, and at the end of the day, I hand them back to the children. That's a signal we're going to Afternoon Wrap-Up soon and starting our home-school connection.

⭐ **If somebody arrives at school and doesn't have his own folder, you don't give up easily on that.** You don't say, "Okay, well, bring it tomorrow. You'll just have to carry your mail home." Tell him, "This is an important part of our community. If you're in my class, you need to have your folder. If you don't have your folder, then you need to borrow one of mine." Emphasize the importance of returning the folder. Send a note to the parents to remind them to try to locate the original folder! It's our way of communicating.

There are lots of different opportunities to use your home-school folders. They could have sheet protectors on the brads with a calendar of events for the month, which would assist the family in looking ahead to events that they might want to participate in. You might put a list of ways to help your child in school or a simple explanation of a strategy for learning that they can be using at home. The folders could hold an agenda for the week or month or even have the students' out-the-door slips for a quick formative assessment at the end of the day. But the important thing to remember is that however you choose to set up the folders, you need to do it in a way that helps the children organize their day so that it becomes a part of the routine.

Getting Ready

Pairing Up

It can be helpful for community-building to pair children for Morning Meeting and Afternoon Wrap-Up so that they all have opportunities to not only get to know one another, but to work with one another. As they enter the room, have a way to pair children available so that they can find and identify their partner prior to joining the group. This practice encourages all children to interact, not just with friends, but at some point with all the children in the class.

You can use two decks of cards and have children find the classmate with the same card, or you might use another simple matching activity, but I much prefer a learning activity. If you take craft sticks and put concepts on them, pairing can become practice. Start with as many craft sticks as you have children in the class. Select a skill, such as matching upper and lower case letters. Label half the sticks with upper case letters and the other half with lower case. Put the sticks in a can and have children draw one as they enter the room. The child with *A* matches with the child with *a*. If one stick has *10 x 4 = ?*, then the matching stick would have *40*. You could have contractions by putting "they will" on one stick and "they'll" on another. You can use facts, shapes, word rules, etc. to match children and practice concepts.

> **Make partner pairing a practice opportunity. Split concepts between pairs of craft sticks and have children find their match.**

Keep in mind that each child needs to sit next to her partner at Morning Meeting and Afternoon Wrap-Up that day. Each day it will be different, so in one of your first lessons on community in whole group, have children brainstorm how to treat others. Teach them how to work with someone who may or may not be their friend.

Have them model appropriate and inappropriate behavior for partner time. All of these types of lessons ensure that the community functions at an optimal level of learning.

When Children Come In at Different Times

In most classrooms, children don't arrive all at once. They may come in on different buses; they may be part of the breakfast program; they may go to an enrichment program before they get to your class. That's reality. Be proactive and have a plan for dealing with that time that lets you turn it into learning time, even though not everyone is there yet.

This is the time when the children turn over their home-school folders and get unpacked. After that, you might have the children who get there early start on morning work. ⭐ **If you can use that morning work to reinforce or review what they learned yesterday, or to help them anticipate what's going to happen today, then you've turned that time into learning time.** It can also be a time for a quick formative assessment that lets you know which children have gained a concept and which ones need additional guided or independent practice.

If you have workstations or centers in your classroom, you might encourage the children to return to those and finish whatever didn't get done yesterday. You might let them use games or puzzles that are fun but that also help reinforce some basic concepts. Or you might have them work on a riddle of the day or a quick research question. Maybe it is something that they can share at Morning Meeting. Get them focused on something that will tie into what the class is going to be doing that day.

The Signal

Once all the children have arrived, you need a signal to start Morning Meeting. It can be a bell. It can be clapping in time while chanting "Morning Meeting, Morning Meeting." Or it can be a song. Children need to know that when the song ends, they should be in a certain area for the meeting. Give them a few seconds to finish what they're doing. Otherwise, you'll get someone like Jeremy, who says, "I was just trying to get that word and now you're bugging me!" They need a signal so that they know they have a couple of seconds to finish up what they're doing and come to Morning Meeting.

Morning Meeting Song

(To the tune of "Where is Thumbkin?")

Where are the students? Where are the students?
It is time. It is time.
Time for Morning Meeting, time for Morning Meeting!
Join us now. Join us now.

Where is _____? Where is _____?
It is time. It is time.
Time to come on over, time to come on over!
Join us now. Join us now.

In the second verse of the song, of course, you insert the name of the last straggler!

You don't have to use the same signal every day. You need to decide: What am I comfortable with? Is it important to my children this year that the signals always remain the same? Will I get the best results from them if it's always the same? Or can I vary the signal, making it more fun to get there because the children can handle that this year? You decide what's best for your class, knowing that what works this year may not be the same thing that worked last year. It all depends on the children.

Remind the children that they are to sit with their partners. Their partner is the person who has the matching card or stick chosen when they arrived this morning. It takes practice, but once the routine is established, students truly understand that everyone is part of the community. We don't always sit with just our friends; we all work together in the community.

> **Create a signal to start Morning Meeting, but allow a few seconds for children to finish what they're doing.**

Morning Greeting

Now the children are all in the same area for Morning Meeting. The first thing we do there is greet each other. I think it's really important to get children talking to other children, to build that classroom community, and to build communication skills. ⭐ **It's very hard for a child to bully another child he's just shaken hands with and said good morning to.** You greeted them at the door, but it's important to have them greet one another, too. I ask every child to greet his partner. Sometimes I tell the children they can use any one of the "three Hs": a handshake, a high five, or a hand wave. That gives children a choice: If I don't want to touch you, I don't have to touch you. I can wave. If you don't want to use the three Hs, you can use made-up rhymes. I like this one:

> *Good morning, friend.*
> *Good day to you.*
> *Hope you have fun today*
> *In all you do!*

A favorite way of doing Morning Greeting is to turn it into a game I call "Attendance-Go-Round." The game works like this: I start things off. I might say, "Good morning, Amy." And Amy says, "Good morning, Mrs. Whyte." The children need to be listening because then I'm going to say, "Good morning, Susan." Susan isn't going to say, "Good morning, Mrs. Whyte"; she's going to say, "Good morning, Amy." She has to go back to the name of the person before her. Then I say, "Good morning, Michael." And Michael is supposed to say, "Good morning, Susan." We keep going that way until everybody's had a chance. I pick names randomly. I don't go in any order, so they don't know who'll be next.

When we play this game, I try to emphasize eye contact so that children learn aspects of communication that build relationships. I teach social skills in there, too. If I start off saying, "Good morning, Amy," and Amy says, "Yeah," I say, "No, that's not okay, Amy; that is not how we greet people." I get a chance to correct communication in social settings. So then I say, "Good morning, Amy." And she needs to reply, "Good morning, Mrs. Whyte."

> **Use Attendance-Go-Round as a morning greeting to keep children engaged and connected.**

Talking Sticks

Over the years it dawned on me why we do not let many children participate in small-group activities: we are afraid to lose control of the group. We worry that one child will monopolize the time we have or that we might never get them all back to listen to us. ⭐ **Truth is that I have found that children who actively participate actually become less of a disruption to the group.** *We* say that they talk too much. I asked myself, "When do I ever give them opportunities to talk? Or is there just too much of an expectation that they are just listeners?" Children can't become good communicators without practice. Collaboration is based on communication. Therefore, if they lack these skills, don't shy away from these activities. Instead, plan to teach the skills.

One of my first lessons involves Talking Sticks, 10-inch-long dowels that I buy in the craft section of a large box store. I decorate one end with ribbon and sometimes even put a bit of glue on the last inch or so and dip it in glitter to make it look like a magic stick. I explain to the students that learning the rules of conversation may require a concrete reminder of our roles. One partner in each of my pairs comes to meeting times with her stick. We can trade off which partner brings the stick each meeting time. Partner A brings the stick in the morning, Partner B in the afternoon.

The stick is in the hand of the person doing the talking, thus the name Talking Stick. The partner without the stick becomes the listener. Set a time limit for sharing answers, such as 30 seconds. Tell the first person to take 15 seconds to share, blow the whistle, and say "switch" so that the children give the sticks to their partners. It is now their turn to be the talkers. It is amazing how teaching children to use the visual of the sticks as a reminder truly keeps them quiet while another person is speaking.

> **Use Talking Sticks to teach children to take turns speaking with a partner. Teach nonverbal cues for listeners to use.**

I also teach them to use nonverbal signals when a person is speaking so they don't interrupt their partner's thoughts. They can shake their heads, raise their eyebrows, even use their hands or the shape of their mouths to show their reaction to what's being said, but they can't talk when the other person has the stick. This activity alone can change the amount of communication in your classroom and teach collaboration skills.

At the beginning of the year, brainstorm what role each person has and what that role "looks like." ⭐ **It is best not to assume that children know how to speak with one another and understand that there are rules to having a constructive conversation. Teach these things.** Show them what it *doesn't* look like in the lesson to ensure that the expectations for both the speaker and the listener are clear. We are always saying that children don't listen. Let's teach them the traits of good listening. When the whole group comes back together, say to the children, "Tell me what your partner shared." I can't tell you how many times a child has said, "Uhmmm, I can't remember, but I said . . . ." I remind the children that I want to understand what their partners shared because it ensures that we build collaborative partners who are good listeners. This is a life skill that will take them very far!

Morning Message and So Much More!

After the greeting, all sorts of things can go on in Morning Meeting. Remember the five components of literacy learning—reading, writing, listening, speaking, and viewing information? It is pretty easy to work every one of them into Morning Meeting every single day. Or I could choose to focus on addressing something that we did yesterday that is related to one of the components. For this, I use some type of an interactive chart, which could be paper, whiteboard, or an interactive whiteboard. By writing and reading with the children, I can review what we covered the day before.

Also, I can easily assess what the children have learned and what has gone over their heads. I could introduce new ideas, give them a chance to practice, and extend or enrich concepts they've already mastered. I could play off the activity to cover standards and build problem-solvers. The opportunities are truly endless. And it can be fun and interactive for the children!

> **An interactive chart, whether it is paper, whiteboard or interactive whiteboard, is a key tool for literacy learning in Morning Meeting.**

The Message

I think it's important to begin the day with a shared literacy activity. I don't know whether you want to write a Morning Message, and I don't want to back you into a corner. Use whatever works for you. If you don't use a Morning Message, maybe you could share a poem. Maybe there's something already on the chart that you'd like to share instead. It might be something that you wrote yesterday with the children, something important enough that it needs to be addressed with the entire class, an activity that needs to be finished, or maybe a graphic organizer. It just needs to be some kind of interactive chart that you can refer back to. The chart activity will allow shared reading and writing to occur during meeting time. Here are a couple of examples:

This is from the beginning of the year for young students. On this chart I could ask partners to talk about letters, high-frequency words, punctuation, or spelling.

> *September 1, 2015*
>
> *Dear Smarties,*
> *Good morning! Today is Tuesday. We have a lot of learning to do today.*
> *Love,*
> *Mrs. Whyte*

This one is for older students. In this case, I have turned my chart into a problem-solving activity for the students.

> *Dear Smarties,*
> *You and your partner are word detectives. Tell me how many words you can make using the letters I M S S A T E R. Try to figure out the mystery word that uses all the letters. How does doing an activity like this one help us to become better readers and writers?*
> *Love,*
> *Mrs. Whyte*

⭐ **The important thing is that you take advantage of using this group time to write *for* and *with* the children. You want to read *with* them. You want to read *to* them. And at some point you want to have them read *by themselves*.** The chart gives you a chance to model whatever it is that you want the children to practice or whatever you believe that they need to become better readers and writers.

Some teachers like to write out a Morning Message ahead of time and then go over it with the children. I used to do that. For the first few years I taught, I ran into school, got my coffee, ran into the room, and wrote a message as fast as I could—before the children got there. I was missing a wonderful opportunity to write *with* the children, to give them a model of what writers think and do. What if you can't think of something to write about? You might say out loud that you tend to think of things you like, don't like, or that are important to you. You might say, "I really want to write that word, but I don't know how to spell it. Where am I going to find out how to spell that word?" When you do it *with* the children, you're the model for how they're going to find that information in the classroom.

⭐ **Model your thinking so they learn to share their thinking out loud.**

Another day, maybe I'd model how you get started with writing when you're stuck: "I'm not sure how to start. Well, I know one way to get started is to think about who I'm writing about, or what I'm writing about, or where something happened." You teach them to think of the five Ws (who, what, when, where, or why) or to think about how something happened. You can model informational writing—how to, descriptive, or persuasive writing. There are so many opportunities, and that is why writing the message *with* the children is so important.

I write the message, share a problem, or teach a concept with the children. I start with the real little ones in kindergarten and first grade, making my writing so repetitive that everyone's going to read it successfully. To become readers, they need to believe they're readers. I always start my Morning Message in the same way: I write the date, and then I write, "Dear Smarties." Every child in my kindergarten class, once he can write letters, starts writing that word *smarties* right away. Once the children have seen it day after day for three or four weeks, every one of them thinks, "Hey, I know how to write that!"—or at least, "I know where to find it." And they copy it—onto whiteboards, onto envelopes, onto index cards, etc. It's important for them to feel that "I know a word. I can write it."

> **Start each Morning Message the same way: include the date, and a consistent greeting.**

In the older grades, let the student teacher write a message or give a problem to solve, which allows partners to work together. Many times my entire grammar lesson can be done in the morning. I will write a sentence that has grammatical errors and have partners "fix it up." Then, I can quickly assess who can and who cannot follow an activity based on the learning concept and begin to excuse the ones "who get it." That allows me to have more time to work with the ones who don't. ⭐ **No one who has driven for years wants to be taught how to drive a car; don't force children who know information to listen to what they already know.** Don't keep everyone at Morning Meeting if they are already able to do the lesson.

Code It with Color

Choral or Echo reading is an absolute must for beginning readers to build confidence. Morning Message is perfect for this. If you're going to write a message with some repetitive language, like "Run, run, as fast as you can," change the color of the marker you use when you get to that language. Or use highlighting tape or the highlighting feature to color it. That way every child feels like "Okay, I don't know what the words say, but I know that when teacher gets to that pink one, I'm going to say, 'Run, run, as fast as you can!'" And then everybody's part of it, and they all experience success. It's the beginning of being able to track print.

In first, second, and third grade, the student teacher might write the message. This encourages them to share things that are important to them and to use tools that you have placed in the classroom, perhaps an anchor chart, word wall, or dictionary for assistance in writing. Teach them to color or highlight parts of language or their writing that they want to share with the group.

In my class, I used green for the beginning; it could be the beginning word, letter, or sentence. We used red for the ending, which could be the punctuation, adding endings to words, or looking at the ending sentence in a paragraph. Purple was our "awesome vocabulary" color. Instead of using a common word, a student would look for an "upgrade" to the word. For example, if the student was going to write, "Mr. Tourville is a very good reading teacher," they would cross out *very good* and above it with the purple marker put the word *stupendous*. This allows students to work on building vocabulary each day. This is also a stupendous opportunity to work on academic vocabulary with your students. Academic vocabulary is used across grade levels and across academic areas of learning. Let's show students the importance of these words in our conversations and written messages.

> **Use color to emphasize elements of the message. Try using green for the beginning, red for the ending, and purple for upgraded vocabulary words.**

Repetition Leads to Success

I always start with the date at the top of my message, but I write it in different ways. I might start by writing, "September 1." Later, I might abbreviate the month and say, "Do you think Mrs. Whyte's tricking you, or did I spell it wrong?" Eventually, I'll use numbers, such as "9/1/15." And I'll ask the children, "Did I make a mistake here?"

> For each Morning Message, consistent elements include the date, a greeting, and a writing or reading opportunity.

Some children will get that in kindergarten. I can still see my Amanda, the child who was way ahead of everybody else. She came to kindergarten, and she was at a second-grade reading level. She knew her way around the library. She'd had more adventures than anybody I knew. She told me what to do most of the time. And then there was Nico. He was on a permanent "in-school field trip;" he just wandered around all the time. These two children were so different in their abilities to take in information. Amanda would be considered gifted and talented. Nico would be considered the slow learner in the class. They both benefited from coming to Morning Meeting and watching me write the date in our Morning Message.

Within a week, Amanda had "gotten it" and understood that I was using an abbreviation for the month. She knew it; she whipped it off; she'd mastered it. It was going to take Nico a lot longer to grasp the concept of multiple ways to write the date. We never know when something's going to click for children. What we need to do is keep putting it out there. It will click when they're ready for it to click, but we need to keep offering those basic concepts in multiple ways. Just remember to send the children who have mastered a concept off to an activity at their learning level.

Those are the starting points. Every day I'd repeat the date, a greeting, and a type of writing or reading opportunity. You may want to focus on different things. You may want to use a different format. Do whatever works for you and your children. Just keep it simple in the beginning, and keep repeating things, so that all the children can succeed. By third grade, you might have totally handed over the chart to the students, and it is great to see them share what they have learned about reading and writing. Just as important is how they learn to communicate and to work with one another.

Opportunities for Formative Assessment

Your Morning Message can be something you and the children write together as a group, whether or not you are the conductor or one of the children is. You or the leader can begin the message, and the group can be working with you. You might even have each of your partners share a whiteboard so that they can show you what they believe the answers to questions are. This is a great and simple formative assessment opportunity. Formative assessment allows you to quickly observe who is with you and who is not.

> Use a
> "signal stick"
> for easy formative
> assessment.

As educators, each of us has lived with the massive amounts of summative assessment placed on our students. Summative assessment measures the student at the end of a course of study to see if he has grown. ⭐ **Formative assessments allow us to modify our teaching in a way that helps each student to grow. This type of assessment takes place day in and day out, allowing us to focus on the learner and his needs.** The most successful meetings take advantage of formative assessment opportunities to gather as much information about the learners as possible. It enables us to spend our time on quality teaching and strategies for individual learners.

Nonverbal responses teach children to self-assess. There may be times when you ask children if they understand a concept that you have introduced or practiced, and they use a simple "signal stick," a craft stick with a green dot on one side and a purple dot on the other, to respond. The green means, "I get it!" The purple means, "I am still confused or don't understand." This helps you, as their teacher, quickly identify who may need additional support. It is important that children learn that they don't have to worry about everyone else's response; this is for just you and them.

Fun (!) with Standards

I think that sometimes teachers get a little overwhelmed with the idea of a Morning Message because there are so many things you can do with it. They're not sure where to go next. I always tell teachers, "Don't try to focus on everything all at once." If you're not sure exactly what you want to include in your Morning Message, take another look at the standards and your curriculum.

Ask yourself if there are on-going standards that need to be exemplified daily in reading and/or writing? Think about directionality. Think about punctuation and grammar. Think about word usage.

Go through the list and think, "How could I address this in a Morning Meeting chart?" Always play off the basics that are foundations to the learning of the individual standards.

Write Aloud

Whenever you write with the children, try to speak out loud. Many of our students do not have a *writer's voice* that operates in their head; someone needs to teach them how writers think. We do this by simply speaking out loud about the challenges writers face. For example, spacing is a basic problem for new writers. You could jam your words together as you write the message, and then start reading them with no breaks between the words. When you write the interactive chart in the morning, the children might say to you, "Molly's the student teacher today." So you start writing that. And you say, "Oh, boy, sometimes when I start writing, I really get going and it gets a little messy. All of my words end up on top of each other. Oh, no. What's the problem

> **Remember to speak out loud whenever you write with children to help them understand how writers think.**

with this? I don't even know where my words begin or end, do I? How am I going to read it? I don't know whether the *S* goes with the *T* or what. How would I know that?"

You can do it in a fun way. If I see a child struggling with spelling a word during journal time, then the next morning in Morning Meeting, I'll model the choices we have when we don't know how to spell a word that we want to use in writing. I might say, "Well, you guys, I want to use the word *fabulous*, but I am not sure how I would spell that." Or I could write something and then say, "Hmmm, do all of you think this looks right? On your board, show me how you think it should be spelled and tell your partner how you knew that." I'm just modeling the same thing that they need to do each day in their own writing.

> **Look at standards for second and third grade that outline revision and editing. These are easily incorporated into shared writing.**

Look at standards for second and third grade that outline revision and editing. These are easily incorporated into shared writing. If you wrote a couple of sentences or a paragraph, you can then go back and ask the children to share with their partners how the writing can be improved for better understanding or better visual imagery.

Many standards for K–3 include, "With guidance and support from adults and peers . . . ." Morning Message is a fantastic opportunity for students to gain that support. If some of the children have a firm grasp on revising and editing when you ask them to share, then release those children from the meeting and spend some quality time giving another example to those who are in need of assistance. I find that teachers who speak out loud about writing to our youngest students provide numerous opportunities for children to achieve the standards. You are teaching, and children are learning to use a "writer's voice."

How Do You Build
Sight-Word Vocabulary?

Long before the new standards, we've known the importance of teaching sight words. I've always felt that if children could master basic words, they'd feel as though they could read. There are various lists, but only one list places the words in order by frequency—the Fry list compiled by Dr. Edward Fry. The first 100 words on the list are reported to make up close to 50% of what we read each day. It is imperative that children master these words. So I want to look for opportunities to say, "Hey, has anybody seen this word before? It happens to be one of our sight words this week. Where would I find it if I didn't know how to spell it?" Then I would ask, "Why is it important to know this word?"

Now that's a lot of words, but if you have to teach that many, I think there's a better way than having children memorize flash cards. Many of us know that although we can get our children to say the words when we flash them, not many can transfer those words from isolation to real reading. I like to concentrate instead on exposing children to those sight words in context all the time. You can use Morning Message to build visual recognition by exposure, to show children how often those words appear. Try using a highlighter or highlighting tape. Ask the partners to talk about/show you which words in the Morning Message are sight words you're working on. Or try leaving out one of those words in Morning Message. Write the message without using the word *the*, and show the children what happens. Or see how often the same word can be included in a paragraph without sounding silly. There are so many opportunities for those words to keep popping up. We need to take advantage of those opportunities. Keep track of the ones the students have mastered, and focus on the ones that most of them still need to learn.

> **Use Morning Message to build visual recognition of sight words by repeated exposure in context.**

More Standards You Can Address with Interactive Charts

Here are just a few of the things that may be on your list of standards. Any of them can be practiced, enriched, maintained, and mastered by your children if you use some type of interactive reading and writing with your students.

- **Consonants and vowels**
- **Sounds** (beginning and ending sounds, blends, and digraphs)
- **Directionality**
- **Syllables**
- **Punctuation**
- **Letters, words, sentences, and symbols**
- **Spacing**
- **Sight words**
- **Rhyming**
- **Friendly letter format**
- **Contractions**
- **Compound words**
- **Root words, prefixes, and suffixes**
- **Synonyms, antonyms, and homonyms**
- **Irregularly spelled words**

Let's say that you choose to teach punctuation in Morning Message. If you use quotation marks every day to identify what somebody said, chances are you won't ever have to teach a formal lesson on quotation marks. The children start to use them because they see *you* use them. You might say, "Well, when somebody says something, we put that in what today? Quotation marks." Put them up there and you'll be amazed: if you say something often enough, you'll see the children starting to get it—when they are ready. ⭐ **When you repeat for the children and you model for them, you give everybody a chance.** To me, this is so much better than saying, "I taught quotes the 3rd of October, and I guess some children didn't get them . . . ."

Remember: use the standards within your meeting so that you can quickly introduce or reintroduce them in a way that allows you to assess the students. You might include a longer word in your Morning Message. Then say, "Let's take this word apart." And you show the children how to break *au/to/mo/bile* into syllables so that they can figure out the word. Then you can offer them a word to work on with their boards and watch to see which students are able to take the word apart and which students struggle. If irregularly spelled words are a challenge for your students, go out of your way to use those words, and it will transfer to the children's writing. The more they see the word spelled, the better visual recognition and automatic recall for the word they will have. This will allow you to work smarter, not harder.

Make Mistakes!

Show your students that spotting mistakes and correcting them are how we learn. Children love it when you make mistakes. I always blame it on the coffee. I say, "You know, Mrs. Whyte didn't have her second cup of coffee, and I think I might have made a mistake here. Does anyone see any problems with this message?" The children will start to pick them out. It's important for them to see how language looks. ⭐ **Editing requires *seeing* that something is not right in your writing.**

You might write *teecher* and say, "Why can't this be the way we spell *teacher*? We learned yesterday that *ee* sounds like this. Why can't it be *t-e-e-c-h-e-r?* It looks like *teacher* to me!" But it just doesn't happen to be the way that particular word is spelled. It doesn't follow that rule you set; it may follow a different rule, or none at all. Take this time to point out the exceptions to the rules we teach, thus allowing children to identify those words and also learn that the rules don't always work in our language.

Some teachers tell me they don't want to write an interactive chart in front of the children. They're worried about what would happen if they made a mistake and had to start over. But what's the message you're sending to the children then? ⭐ **Be the model that teaches students to move on and not focus on a mistake.** I think if you make a mistake, you should have white sticky notes or some of that big white tape that comes from the dollar store—somebody referred to it once as "boo-boo tape"—and you should say, "Oh! Giant white-out!" Just stick that tape on there and write over the mistake. Say, "I'm so glad I wasn't worried about that! Worrying wouldn't have solved this problem!" Don't be surprised if, during a writing center or journal time, someone asks for the boo-boo tape!

What If They Don't Find the Mistakes?

Sometimes it's a good idea to make a mistake without pointing it out to the children. You hope that someone will identify it. But what if they don't? Don't sweat it! You're trying to challenge the learners who can go there, who can spot the mistakes, and who can learn from them. But if they don't all get there, that's fine. Don't worry about it. Just try it again another day.

Are You Including Everyone?

The way you ask a question can either be inclusive, or it can leave children out. My biggest concern is the children who are left out.

What's the Question?

Research shows that when you talk to a group of children, you can plan on only some of the group taking in what you say. They understand it, and they're actually paying attention. That's the top two percent. Then you have this middle group: they do understand it, but they're not really paying attention. So some of it goes in; some of it goes out; it's kind of a mishmash. That's the whole bell curve in the middle. Then there are these little guys at the other end: They might even be looking at you and smiling. They're not listening to a darned thing you say. The reality is that they're over there in their own little world.

   I left children out—never on purpose, never meaning to, but I didn't think about it. I left them out because I pointed to the writing and said things like "Who can find the sight words on this interactive chart?"

> Well, I'm very sorry, Amy. You don't even know what a sight word is. You call them "word-wall words," so when I change it to "sight words," you don't know what I'm asking for. You, Christopher, you know one sight word, but it's not the one on the chart. Nathan knows sight words, but he doesn't talk, so he's not going to raise his hand. It's not in his personality. And Jennifer is the show-off. She's got her hand up. She knows every sight word on there. She can read the whole chart. But she doesn't need to because Jennifer is the child in the two percent. She's the only one I really included. Unfortunately, she is the child that doesn't even need the lesson.

We assume, "Gee, they got all the directions. I gave them those directions." But it's not that simple. I think of my Courtney. One day I sat with her at a center. I was trying very hard to get her to focus, and I said, "Courtney, do you get it, hon?"

She said, "Yes."

I said, "Then repeat it back to me."

And she said, "What's that in your teeth?"

She didn't get it because that's not where her focus was—it wasn't on the words. So we have to be careful of that, remembering that some of them are going to pick up some of what we say, and very few are going to get all of it.

Everyone's Invited

I've been in many classrooms where I've heard teachers asking questions the way I did until a mentor teacher mentioned a better method to me. ⭐ **If I change the way I question the children in my classroom, I open the lesson up to all of the children.** We need to be cautious with closed-ended questions. Instead, train yourself to ask things like, "Hey, guys, what do you notice about Mrs. Whyte's chart today?" Everybody's invited. If a child is quiet, I might need to call on him and recognize that. But when you put it in that kind of language, you'll be surprised. When I started doing it, part of me was always thinking, "Oh, my gosh, am I going to get through this day?" But you'd be amazed what a difference the language makes. It invites children into the community instead of pushing them out. Take those opportunities to question children in a way that opens it up to them.

The first time I ever said, "What do you notice about this chart?" little Ryan raised his hand. Ryan was never one of the children in that top two percent, so I was thinking, "What did Ryan notice?"

And he said, "I noticed it's a little messy."

"It's messy? Ryan, what's messy?" ⭐ **What you need to do as a teacher is say, "How do I turn what he just said into my next lesson?"**

My next lesson was, "What's messy? The top? Or the bottom?" (Point to those parts of the chart as you say the words.)

"The bottom, Mrs. Whyte."

I'd been sitting in a chair and writing, and in fact, when I got to this part of the chart, I did kind of go off to the side. So I knew which part he thought was messy. But I said, "Is it a word? Or is it the whole sentence that you think is messy?"

He said, "Just the end."

I said, "So it's this word. Do you know what this word is?" You can play off what they say, no matter what it is, to teach them something else.

You can get into trouble with this. You'd better be on your toes. I had a wall in my classroom that had nothing but children's names on it; we played off children's names—children love that. We'd count the letters, compare who had how many letters, who had which sound at the beginning, what their names ended with. I sent Cody to the word wall during Morning Meeting one day, and I said, "Cody, bring me two names that are different—not the same, different." And he came back with the names *Katy* and *Cody*.

Then I thought, "How are these two names different? Okay, they both have four letters. Cody's that child who doesn't really know his letters yet, so it's not the letters and sounds that he's looking at. He must be counting the letters. But they have the same number of letters, so it can't be that. What could it be? He chose his name and then a little girl . . . hmmm. I'm thinking he's going to say something about the first letter of each name. I just know it."

The easy way to find out what he was thinking was just to say, "Cody, how are these two names different?" And he said, "One's a girl, and one's a boy." That was true. Then I said, "Yes. And notice there's a *y* in each name, and there are four letters in each name. One starts with *C* and one starts with *K*; sometimes these letters sound similar—tell your partner if they sound similar in these names."

Then, I sent Cody back to the word wall later that day. I said, "This time, Cody, when you come back, I want to see two names that are the same. Okay? Cody, get two that are not different." And he came back. This time the two names were *Jeremiah* and *Ann*. What was the same about those two names? I thought, "It has to be the *A*. If he recognizes a capital versus a lowercase *A*, he must be looking at the *A*." If I wanted to know, I had to ask him, "Cody, how are these two names the same?"

He said, "I don't like either one of those names."

"Why don't you like those names, Cody?"

"Because *Jeremiah* takes too long to write, and *Ann* is no fun because it only has three letters."

You have to be prepared for the answers. You need to be able to teach off those, and sometimes it's tough. How are you going to teach off that? I'm locked into one lesson and he's locked onto something else entirely. He's going in a different direction. I need to then take what he says and figure out how I can turn it into a lesson for him. So I might then say, "Cody, Jeremiah's name has a lot of sounds in it. When there are a lot of sounds, there are a lot of letters. Can you help me count how many letters each name has?"

By then, Ann is crying, "He doesn't like my name!" So that might turn into its own lesson. But the reality is, we don't know what's in children's heads. And so the way we question them is really important. I think the way we question children in Morning Meeting and Afternoon Wrap-Up is huge. Could I teach off it? Yes. Was it what I was expecting? Absolutely not.

Questions to Grow On

When you get children to discover a concept for themselves, or teach from a concept that they choose, they hang onto it. They think they discovered it. But you've got to get them there by asking the right questions. Here are some to try:

- What do you notice?
- Can anyone tell me anything about this _____?
- Does anything on the chart/in the picture/in the writing make you think of something in your life?
- What part did you spot?
- What do you think?
- Do you see something (different, familiar, weird, etc.)?
- What do you recognize?
- Can you tell me what you see?
- Can you show me something on the chart?
- What do you know about this (chart, calendar, book)?
- Does anyone have any ideas about _____?

Maybe this is a day when we look at vocabulary in the message, "What do we really mean when we say 'a week has flown by'?" Another day, maybe somebody has a new baby in the family. I might write, "Five children is a big family. How many children are in your family?" Here again, each child can share with a partner. Then I might ask which is the "most common number" in our class families or the "smallest number versus the largest number" of people in a family. ⭐ **Choose carefully the way you talk to and question your children. It could mean the difference between them actually learning a concept or just listening to you.** You might add a question about why it's good to have lots of siblings or what might be some of the challenges. Being able to justify an answer plays a huge role in the new comprehension standards.

> **Remember to ask open-ended questions whenever possible.**

No More Hand-Raising

Every teacher of elementary children is astutely aware of a problem that we create. Whenever we say, "Children, I have a question for you," every hand in the room goes up before we have even asked the question. Why? Because children learn quickly that the rule is, if I want to talk or be involved, I must get my hand in the air as quickly as possible. ⭐ **Therefore, the school system creates children who don't think, but instead raise hands and wave as soon as they feel a question is coming.** We've all asked those children to respond when they haven't even heard the question; most say, "uhmmm . . . I forgot" or "once my grandmother told me . . . ." They all want to be involved, and most want to talk, but they're totally off-task. The truth is that once we choose the child to answer from the hands that were waved, most other children aren't even involved any longer.

> **Morning Meeting and Afternoon Wrap-Up are times for Turn and Talk. Whenever a question is asked, give the children time to turn and talk. Then have them share with the larger group, so everyone gets to participate.**

Remember to tell your class that there is no hand-raising during Morning Meeting and Afternoon Wrap-Up. Explain that this is a place where communication is shared and that the class will be learning listening and speaking skills all year long. Each day they will be expected to speak with and listen to their partner of the day. Whenever a question is asked, give the children time to turn and talk. Ask them to share their thoughts and ideas about the question posed. This should be a quick turn and talk. Have a consistent signal for when the time is over; I use a train whistle. Once the children are back with you, choose a person at random to tell you what her partner told her. It truly teaches children to become better listeners and responders.

The "Me" Folder

We need to understand that children are coming to school with "me" folders. It's all about "me." It really is, when you're young. If it's not about you, then you want to know, "How is it related to me?" To a young child, if it's not about them, it's probably not important. ⭐ **We need to build on the "me" folder and get them thinking in broader terms about "How do these things that I'm learning relate to me?"** Keep it personal. Help children make connections between themselves and what they learn, what they read, and the world around them. The more Morning Message is about them, or they see relevant learning in it, the more likely you're going to connect with them.

Calendar Time

Graphic organizers are nothing new—we were using them long ago. One of the first was a calendar. Anybody who's ever counted to 100 days of school has seen an opportunity to teach math with the calendar. There are all kinds of ways you can use a calendar to teach. So bring your calendar into Morning Meeting.

> **Your calendar is the basis for activities to build number sense, to assess children's understanding, and to remediate.**

Intervention

In kindergarten, and in first, second, and third grades, calendar time can become intervention time. Use your calendar every morning to review basic math concepts, and assess who understands them. Send those students who do understand off to work on something else; keep the children who need remediation in the meeting, and use the calendar as a way to review and reteach concepts.

Odd and Even

To teach odd and even, alternate colors on the numbers of the calendar. "Can somebody show me an odd number here? An even number? What's my hint? That's right: Can I share with a friend and have the same amount, or will there be leftovers? If there are leftovers, is it an odd number or an even number? That's right: it's an odd number."

Buy or make cutouts of cookies. Start with three "cookies." Ask the children, "If I take one and you take one, do we have any left over? Does that mean that three is an even number or an odd number?" You can repeat this with much higher numbers.

Riddles

You can make up little riddles about today's date. That's one the children like because they know what the question is going to be. They can get prepared before they come. If today were the ninth, I might say, "I'm looking for a problem that has something to do with nine."

And somebody might say, "9 plus 0."

"That would be 9. Anybody have a different one?"

"8 plus 1."

"8 plus 1 would be 9."

There are lots of different ways to get to 9. This lets all children respond no matter what their abilities. It helps you assess what they've learned.

Number sense includes understanding that numbers are everywhere, and they can be represented in many different ways. If you ask, "What do you notice about this number?" you know what you're going to get? You're going to get little Courtney who says, "Nine! That's in my phone number!" Or "That number's on my house!" That's all she knows. And then you're going to get Amanda, who says, "9 would be 2 times 18 divided by 4." That's where she is. That's okay. It lets everyone bring whatever they know about the number 9. It's important to give children those opportunities to play with numbers and to level your teaching to what they know about a particular number—as opposed to what they don't know. That's one way to play off the calendar every day. You're building number sense.

> **Pose riddles for your students, and encourage them to make up their own. Riddles require synthesis, analysis, and evaluation—all higher-order thinking skills.**

You could also write out a riddle that requires partners to find an answer, such as: "Bobby throws a ball as hard as he can. It comes back to him, even though nothing and nobody touches it. How?" In this way we are creating thinking opportunities where collaboration and communication are required. Riddles require synthesis, analysis, and an evaluation. Wow—higher-level thinking all the way around. By the way—Bobby throws the ball straight up!

Money Concepts

You can have fun with money combinations on a calendar, too. "Today's the 16th. Can anybody show me that in money? What's 16? Is there more than one way to show it?" Maybe Amanda says, "We could use three nickels and a penny." Put the coins in the little flap on the calendar so that you can see them.

Tomorrow, if I'm Stephen and you ask me, "Can you find a way to make 17?" I'm going to say, "Use three nickels, a penny, and add a penny." Because it's one more day. They start to understand that. And then when you run out of pennies you say, "Well, we don't have any more pennies. I guess we can't do this anymore. Can anybody think what we can do?" Maybe we'll trade some of those pennies for a nickel. Just make sure you run out of pennies!

Other Calendar Activities

There are all kinds of other ways you can use calendars to explain basic math concepts. How many of these things are you already teaching with calendars?

Patterning. Many teachers believe that patterning has been eliminated from early math standards—not true. Keep in mind that our entire number system is a pattern. Show the dates in a pattern of red, purple, red, purple, and so on. Ask, "What color do you think will be next?" Or, with older children, look at the pattern in the numbers themselves. "There's a 7. Right under 7 is the number 14. Why is that? What happens when we add another week? That's right: we add seven days."

Building Number Sense. Say to the children, "Show me 9." They can stamp their feet nine times. They can tally nine. They can count out nine stickers or draw nine smiley faces. They can write the word *nine*.

Skip Counting. "Here's 5, and here's 10, and here's 15. Can anybody show me what comes next?" Point out the patterns as you count by twos, threes, or fives.

Geometry. Combine patterning and geometry by marking the dates with geometric shapes. "Oh, the number 1 has a cylinder on it. The number 10 has a cylinder on it. But gee, the number 2 has a triangle, and the number 12 has a triangle. I think I see something similar about these numbers on this calendar." Reinforce the concept of shapes. You might even ask how the shapes are different.

Morning and Nighttime. "We're here in the morning with the calendar. What happens before I see you the next morning? That's right: there's a night."

Time of Day. "Do I see you at 2 a.m.? Why not?"

Yesterday, Today, and Tomorrow. "Today is Wednesday. What was yesterday? What day will tomorrow be?" You're pointing out the circular pattern.

Before and After. "Next Monday is the 10th. What came before the 10th? What comes after it?" You're teaching ordinal numbers, too!

Place Value. "When we get to the 10th number, we have a ones place (the 0) and a tens place (the 1). That's the 0. That's the 1." Using that language helps as you practice place value into the hundreds to count to 100 days of school.

Mathematical Language. "Today is the 12th. Can somebody show me a number that's greater than 12? Can somebody show me a number that's less than 12?" Look for all the opportunities to use the calendar to teach the concepts of greater than and less than, more and less, bigger and smaller, higher and lower.

Sequencing. "We started school on Monday. What day comes after Monday?" "This is October. What month comes after October?"

Graphing. Keep track of the weather on the calendar each day, and then make a graph to show the number of rainy days, the number of snowy days, and the number of sunny days. Graph the number of days in each month.

Seasons. "This is October. What season of the year does October fall into? What season comes next? What do you like or dislike about this season?"

Holidays. "This is December. Can anybody tell me a special holiday that comes this month?"

Once again our best opportunity for learning will come in allowing pairs to work on the above and to share their answer in a quick formative assessment format, thus enabling us to stop working on the concepts that have clearly been mastered by the learners.

Warning!

Many times the calendar becomes a chore that we must do, and it becomes so rote that there is absolutely no new learning involved. Children who know the concept become robotic at repeating answers back to you; children who don't might be overwhelmed by the sheer volume of what we can teach by using a calendar. Try to focus on only one or two concepts a day, thus allowing time for reteaching and practice, as opposed to trying to rush through all the ways you can teach with a calendar. Far too many times I have witnessed the best-intentioned teacher rush through all of the concepts each day. Please remember that the ones who have it don't need to participate, and the ones who don't need us to slow down and do one concept at a time. While there are many opportunities to teach, teach calendar concepts in a way that is beneficial to all students.

The Schedule

You've done Morning Message. You've gotten them up with a song or activity, and now the children are ready to move on. They need a change of pace. They also need to know what's going to happen: "What will I be doing today, and why?" This is when you get to the schedule for the day. The schedule gives you a way to let children know what to expect, what to prepare for, what to look forward to. They like that.

> **Use a pocket chart to create and manage the schedule.**

Changing the Schedule? Warn Those Children!

Just as we do, children need a warning about what's going to happen. It's especially good to forewarn those children who depend on consistency. Always remember to allow for that. If you're going to change the schedule from your usual routine, you'd better let the children know first thing in the morning. In my class, Caitlin was one of those children who needed to be alerted to changes in the schedule. She knew what time lunch was, and if you traded lunch with any other teacher, you'd better let her know because if she didn't know, she was going to wig out when that time came.

The schedule is actually a pocket chart. You can buy them ready-made or make your own. You can use analog "clocks" or you can make little clock faces with the hands on them. However you choose to handle the mechanics, the schedule gives you a great way to teach time every day; it also sets up *what we will do today* for the review in Afternoon Wrap-Up of *what we have done today, and why*.

I made my own pocket-chart schedule, and I made the cards to go into the pockets. It worked like this: We said, okay, around this time we're going to be in Morning Meeting. Then we had literacy time and centers, and after that we had a remedial math teacher. So math had to start when the remedial math teacher came, which meant that math would start at 11:00 a.m. I wanted to make the clock with the little hands show that math was going to begin at 11:00 a.m. That way, a child in the back of the room working in his centers could look at the clock and say, "Uh-oh, I'm going to run out of time here."

I can teach the children to do that: I can teach them to know what the next thing is on the schedule. I can show them about what time it starts. I can show them how to watch for that time on the big classroom clock. I remember sticking highlighting tape on that clock and saying, "When the big hand hits that highlighting tape, you're going to be out of time. So you need to keep track of that hand up there." You're teaching them the beginnings of managing time. You're teaching the children timing—the reality of our lives.

> **Give children a signal before ending an activity, so they have time to finish up their work. Ring a bell, clap, use rain sticks, or flick the lights to remind them to check the clock.**

Sometimes the schedule in my classroom didn't say that we were going to have math at 11:00 a.m. Sometimes it just said that we were going to be doing centers for 20 minutes. So the children had to figure out how long that was and how much time they had left. Use warning signals to remind them to check the time. Maybe you clap, or use rain sticks, or flick the lights. Any of these will help students get the concept of managing their own time.

Telling Time

In every grade, first through third grade, children need to have a chance to practice measuring time. Is it going to be one week in February? Or is it going to be anytime you can bring it up? Make this practice work for you and the children. Maybe today I don't have time in Morning Meeting. I'd love to touch on time, but today I'm working on a couple of other things I have to practice, so I'm just going to tell the children, "This is today's schedule, and you'll note that there's a change right here." I'm not going to refer to the clock.

On other days, when I have the opportunity, I'm going to say, "Why would that big hand be past the 12 like that? Oh, that's because we're not going to go there until five minutes after the hour." You take that opportunity to teach them how to tell time, and the language and vocabulary of time.

But You Promised!

You do have to be careful about how you present the schedule. Never physically write a promise like "Today we're having an assembly" or "Today we're going to . . . " because if that doesn't come true, that's enough to set a little child off. "You said we were!" Can't you just hear them?

I make sure the children understand what I mean when I write, "We're *supposed* to go to an assembly at 2:00 p.m." That way they realize that sometimes we say things in certain ways. It doesn't mean we're promising. We're just saying that that's what we expect to do: "I'm going to give you the schedule today, and as much as I can, I'm going to stick to that schedule. But if something comes up and I don't get to it, sweetie, it's not that I made a promise that I broke. I just didn't get to it. So let me just tell you that this is a tentative schedule. This is what we *might* do today, and I hope we'll get to everything." ⭐ **Be careful with your wording because children take it very literally once you've written it down, and they'll hold you to that "promise."** You give children a format to follow: "Yes, we're going to have to move on." Just make sure you do it without making promises.

Keep in Mind

Here are some practical things to keep in mind as you plan and facilitate your Morning Meetings.

Dealing with School Announcements

Often, it's during Morning Meeting that someone from the principal's office comes over the intercom with announcements for the whole school. Those announcements can be a headache. You don't always know when they're going to come. You don't know how long they're going to last. So what's your plan for dealing with them? Are you going to incorporate them into Morning Meeting? Are you going to wait to start the meeting until the announcements are over? You need a plan.

My plan was always this: I knew that morning announcements would come during Morning Meeting. It might be while a child was talking; it might be while I was talking. So I told the children that as soon as they heard that bell, they needed to "freeze." And I'd model that—I'd show them what it meant to freeze.

> **Formulate a plan to accommodate school announcements. Have students "freeze." Discuss any important information. Use it in the meeting, if it's relevant.**

I think the sad thing is children don't really hear what that person on the intercom is saying. Make it a part of the meeting. Maybe there's nothing important in the announcements. Maybe Mrs. Fletcher says, "Good morning. There will be no soccer practice today." That doesn't even involve us, so it doesn't go to the "me" message. But what if she says, "Mrs. Green is out, and there's no substitute, so there won't be any after-school program today"? That's an important piece of information for us. We need to take in that information and then say, "Well, where do we file information that we hear coming in?"

If it involves your children, you might even say, "Well, what in that announcement concerns us?" Ask the children to share with a partner if it directly affects them. It could also become a creative writing exercise to say, "Where is Mrs. Green today? I bet I know where Mrs. Green is." And I laugh about it. Tell partners to make their prediction of where Mrs. Green is today. Then later in the day the children write about where they think Mrs. Green is. They think she's out to lunch, eating Chinese food.

You Gotta Have Movement!

Never forget that if you want this meeting to hold, you'd better figure out how you're going to move the children every once in a while. You can't expect children to sit all the time. In educational circles, you always hear different theories about how long children can sit still. Many people go by the rule of thumb that the average attention span of a child is his age plus 3 minutes.

We know that that's the *average* child. Now let's talk about the child who's not average. Maybe she came to school at a younger age than her peers. Instead of saying she can sit still for her age plus 3 minutes, you might as well call it her age minus 3 because she's not average. Then you've got the children at the other end. They're not average either. Let's say one of these children is 8. If you add 3, that means you have 11 minutes. But in reality, this child could be good for 20 to 25 minutes if you have something that interests him.

Pick whatever rule of thumb you like. ⭐ **The bottom line is, there's no way you can expect a bunch of children to sit quietly at their desks all morning and still be learning anything.** If I use the "age plus 3" rule and the children in my class are 5, I've got 8 minutes. If I've already used 10 on the interactive reading and writing, I'm beyond time. I'd better move them. Now!

This is when you need a song, a poem, or an exercise activity—anything to get the children moving. Every teacher I know has a collection of these. Brain Breaks are great for this, and you can find a terrific variety online. Project them on your interactive whiteboard. Or you can use an old tune and have the whole class make up new words for it together. It doesn't matter where you get this stuff. I like to keep a folder of the class's favorite songs and poems. Then when the children need some physical activity, I pick a song or poem out of the folder, and we sing or say it together. Or I let the children pick a favorite. Ideally, we sing a song that involves movement or add an activity so that we address our need for movement. If you need something quick and easy, try an activity like Slump or Jump. Have the students stand and ask them questions. If their response is yes, they jump; if their response is no, they slump. This is also an easy formative assessment for who was paying attention during the meeting, and it allows for quick movement.

How Long Is Long Enough?

A major dilemma in teaching surrounds knowing when to move on! Most of the time, Morning Message takes about 7 to 10 minutes. You have time only to touch on the things we've been talking about. But once you get the children involved, it can be great. One teacher in Alaska told me, "Donna, one day I spent an hour and 10 minutes on the message. We wrote four pages. Everyone kept adding things." If you can get that much teaching out of it and the children stay with you, I'd keep going. The minute you start to lose them, cut the message short. It's time to add the period and move on. Maybe it's time for a song or a chant or getting them up to hop for a minute. You need to give them time in between activities. If they're with you, stay with it. If they're not, go on to something else.

If you wonder whether Morning Meeting is worth the time you're taking for it, just list all the opportunities to teach that you can find in having interactive reading and writing opportunities each day. Look at the skills you can teach and think to yourself, "Is this time well spent?" When I asked the teacher in Alaska to do that, she came back with 18 topics that she had covered by using a chart. I said to her, "If you can do that, then I think you spent your time well. You probably did more than some people do in five hours."

A Final Word About Morning Meeting

Connecting Writing and Reading

Don't ever make the mistake of writing without going back and rereading it at the end. Find the time to reread. People don't write and leave it. Good writers go back and review the writing. Now that it's written, it's time for you to read it in its entirety. Or have the children read it in its entirety. Many standards focus on editing and ensuring writing is sending the message that you want. ⭐ **You need to make sure students understand the connection between writing and reading.** You're still modeling good writing. And reading back through the interactive writing task builds language skills and listening skills. It is important that students know that reading and writing are connected and the better you are at one, the better you get at the other.

It Doesn't Have to Be Elaborate

Remember: Morning Meeting is filled with opportunities. Use it to teach and share, but remember that it should always be based on the children and their needs. Being flexible with your goals on any given day will let you gain more teachable moments than you might ever have imagined. It is imperative that this whole-group time focuses on the needs of the individual children and the group within this class. We need to cement our community by meeting together, discussing topics, and addressing concerns. We also need to be aware of how each individual student can benefit from this shared time.

One teacher said to me, "Donna, you think too fast on your feet. I couldn't sit there and think of a lesson off the top of my head." I remember telling her, "I think you're going way too deep. I think you're thinking you need some extravagant lesson. What you need to know are the standards and how to build them into everyday activities." ⭐ **Many of us are so used to offering plans for every second of our day that we fail to recognize that higher learning takes place when we are able to switch gears and address the needs of our children on the spot. And that takes practice on your part!**

For example, a standard that exists in most of the primary grades is "to know and apply grade-level phonics." Every once in a while when we're writing our Morning Message, looking at a poem, or filling in a graphic organizer, I'll talk about a specific phonetic rule within the context of written language. In this way I incorporate the standard into a real writing-reading opportunity. I think sometimes we get too hung up on "What's the lesson?" "When will I have time to teach or reteach that standard?" Bringing in an example can easily allow me to make a quick assessment of the children who are able to follow along and those who are not. Sometimes we don't need an elaborate lesson plan. Sometimes we need to recognize whether children are with us and use what's going on at that "teachable moment." Learn to introduce, practice, and extend concepts by pointing them out in the natural process. Often it is more authentic and effective than waiting for the time you have written in your plan.

PART 4

AFTERNOON WRAP-UP

How It Began

I was a student teacher for a kindergarten one year, and I can remember how excited I was on my first day. The teacher took out the plan book, and all the plans were written so neatly. The plan said, "On Monday, we will do page 100. On Tuesday, we will do page 101. On Wednesday, we will do page 102." And it continued that way, with page 103 on Thursday and 104 on Friday, and so on. Who was going to figure out whether the children ever got page 101 before we took them to the next step? When were we going to do that? Were we going to wait until we tested them two weeks later on the chapter? That doesn't work. Some of these children aren't getting what we're doing on Monday, and we're pushing them on to Tuesday. Then we say, "Gee, you know what? They're really falling behind." We *left* them behind. We left them back there because we didn't know that's where they were.

Afternoon Wrap-Up gives me a chance to evaluate the day. I'm going to be asking the children questions. We're going to be working together on some review activities. I'll find out what they got and what they didn't get so that I know what I need to do tomorrow. We started as a group and learned what we were going to do today; we did it; and now we need to ask, "What did we do and why?"

Putting an End to the "Nothing" Answer

The biggest thing for me as a teacher is to prevent those children from going home and doing what my children did to me as a parent—that is to say, telling me they did "nothing" all day. We hear that way too much. We don't want children who say, "Nothing." We want children who say, "I did this." ⭐ **More importantly, we want children to know why we do the things we do in school—how it relates to their lives and their futures.**

We all know how frustrating it is: You took extra time to prepare. You spent the whole day working hard with the children. They were excited. They were learning. Then the "nothing" answer—Ugh! We need to change that!

First of all, just the way we question children stops them from answering the question. "What did you do in school today?" is too overwhelming to a child. We need to change the way we ask that. Instead, go straight to what I call the "Information Highway for Children." Start with the five senses. Ask, "What did your eyes see in school today?" Can they say, "Nothing"? Not unless they had their eyes closed all day. They must have seen *something*. "Did you see the teacher? Any charts? Anything on the interactive whiteboard?"

"What did you hear at school today?" "Did you hear a new book being read to you? Do you remember what the book was about? Did you learn a new song?"

"Where did your feet take you at school today?" "What did your hands do at school today?" Start asking them specific questions about their senses, and all of a sudden it's easier for them to recall that information and give it back to someone.

You're building associative memory for children. We depend on rote memory way too much in our classrooms: "If I just keep saying it, I bet they'll memorize it." We need to build associative memory that leaves the children saying, "Gee, when she asks, 'What did my hands do?' what I need to do is look at my hands and think about what it is that my hands did." "I need to visualize my hands during the day, and then I'll be able to come up with something." We want to build associative memory in our classrooms.

I used to say to children, "Okay, what's the one thing no one in this class is going to say when they get home today and Mom or Dad says, 'What did you do in school today?'"

They said, "Nothing!"

> **Use questions about the five senses to get them thinking about what happened in school today.**

I said, "That's right. That's against the law. That word is not in our vocabulary. It's not acceptable to say, 'Nothing.' You didn't do nothing. If you did, we made a big mistake. We did lots! So, let's put on our thinking caps and recall the many things we did today".

So in Afternoon Wrap-Up, you're going to be giving children an opportunity to play some review games and discuss their day so that when they go home and their parents ask what they did, nobody will say, "Nothing." And at the same time, you're going to find out what "stuck" for them.

Check In Before Checking Out

You can use Afternoon Wrap-Up in lots of different ways to accomplish lots of different things. ⭐ **Just like we did with Morning Meeting, you need to decide what your goals are for Afternoon Wrap-Up in your classroom; then you can figure out which activities will get you there.** For example, here are some of the goals that I set for our Afternoon Wrap-Up in my classroom.

Overview or Review?

Are you going to do an overview of the day because you think it's important to bring all the pieces together? Or are you going to review? Those are two options during Afternoon Wrap-Up. I hear from teachers, "I like to kind of outline it." Some people think it's really important to connect the dots for children: "During math today we learned about graphing. In science we kept track of temperatures. Let's bring those skills together." That's the person who needs to do the overview. I like a review—from the children's perspective, not from mine. (I'll get to that in a minute.) Maybe you do an overview one day and a review the next.

What Worked and What Didn't?

The overview or review gives you the opportunity to find out what worked and achieved your goals today and, just as important, what didn't. You will know that a lesson didn't work if not one student brings it up. It didn't work if they answer in a way that has nothing to do with the topic. And what if they remember the lesson but think it was about something else entirely? This is something we need to know—in fact, we may need to note that we should find a better or *different* way to teach that lesson tomorrow!

Find Out What Interests the Children

During Afternoon Wrap-Up, I like to ask the children what they think we're going to do the next day. One day we read *If You Give a Pig a Pancake*, and I asked them what they thought we'd do the next day. Of course they all said, "Make pancakes!" ⭐ **Afternoon Wrap-Up gives you an opportunity to listen to what the children say and then extend the lesson in that direction if you can.** Sometimes you can't, but boy, those few times that you can might make all the difference. There are a whole lot of standards you can meet by creating a list of items needed to make pancakes, ordering the steps it takes to make the pancakes, and actually carrying out the task.

Return to the Focus of the Day

Afternoon Wrap-Up can give you a better understanding of how well you met your focus for the day. At the end of the day we shouldn't just say, "What a great day!" We should be able to say, "You know, there was focal point to that lesson. Did they get it?" Maybe the focus was the sequence of the life cycle of a monarch butterfly. When you get to the end of the day and you're doing your review, if the children can show that they understand the cycle and can ask and answer questions about it, then you've achieved the purpose. If they thought the lesson was all about caterpillars, then they may have missed the main idea, and you need to go back to it tomorrow.

Evaluate the Day

Afternoon Wrap-Up gives me a chance to see how each child would evaluate the day. That means I want the student to review what he learned today. And I also want him to review his own role within our classroom community.

Look Forward

I want to give the children a chance to anticipate what we're going to do tomorrow and how it ties in to what we learned today. I want them to learn about setting goals and to understand that our lessons are intertwined and that this learning transfers to their everyday lives.

Have a Closing for the Day

Having a closing routine for the end of the day makes everybody feel like part of the community. And it's nowhere near as stressful as the "Oh-no-the-buses-are-here" alternative!

> **Use Afternoon Wrap-Up to see how each child would evaluate the day. Give children a chance to anticipate what they're going to do tomorrow and how it ties in to what they learned today.**

Intentional Choices

A major goal of my work as a teacher is to build problem-solvers and community—children who think, can communicate, and who collaborate. To build and extend the framework that supports children learning these valuable skills, I must make intentional choices; I must know *why* I do what I do. For example:

Why My Children Were Packed Up by 3:00 p.m.

You can't just wait for the bell to ring and then tell the students they have to leave in 5 minutes. It takes one child 15 minutes to get organized, and it takes another child 2. Jonathan may be all packed up and waiting at the door, and here's Chelsea still looking for her lunch box. ★ **But what you *can* do is organize the end of the day so that the children understand that you can be packed and ready to go home without learning time being over.** The buses arrived at my school at 3:30. I wrapped up my class at 3:00 because there was a lot to do in the review time, and I wanted to be able to use that as teaching time. If it takes the children 10 minutes to pack, then we will have 20 minutes for Afternoon Wrap-Up. If it takes them 25 minutes to pack (those darn winter boots and mittens), then we will only have 5 minutes to wrap up.

> **Set aside the last half-hour of your day for packing up and wrapping up. Pack up first and use what's left to wrap up.**

Remember that we are creating an environment that is based on community. In the Morning Meeting section, I mentioned that we need to treat out students as guests when they arrive, so let's try the same when they leave. We would never say, "Hey, nice to see you; your car is in the driveway," and run them out the door. Our children deserve so much more, and we would miss an awesome opportunity to learn about the day from the most important people in the room—our students.

Why Do the Overview or Review?

The overview or review gives you a chance to figure out how best to continue with lessons. Not that you're not going to do page 102; if that's what's in your lessons, you're going to do it. But the overview or review will give you time to say, "What do I have to do to get ready to teach that next page, if they didn't get all of this the day before?" It gives you a better understanding of the children's point of view of what they did. Sometimes this isn't pretty!

I remember one time I had this great lesson in fractions. I'd asked my husband to cut a wooden circle into eight pieces, and I'd painted all of the pieces in different colors. This was an awesome fractions lesson. I gave the children these colored pieces so that we could study fractions, and I thought this was great. Many times during the day, I had to remind children to share and to move on from our new center—they really liked the wooden pieces, and I was thrilled that the lesson went over so well. Then—we got to the end of the day and Afternoon Wrap-Up. I remember I was at my desk, and my coteacher was running the wrap-up. She said, "I'm wondering whether anyone can think of anything we did in math today that you might want to tell your mom or dad about at home." And I was thinking, "Yeah! Mr. Whyte and I spent all that time on this, and I am sure they will mention the blocks!"

One little girl spoke up and said, "Math? We didn't do math today." And the coteacher said, "I think we did. Does anyone remember?" One of the other children said, "You know, those wooden pieces."

> The overview or review will give you time to say, "What do I have to do to get ready to teach that next page, if they didn't get all of this the day before?"

And the little girl said, "Oh! I thought that was about learning to share the pieces."

You know what? I needed to know that. I needed to know that she hadn't even understood that we were supposed to be playing with those to learn about fractions. ⭐ **You're looking for their point of view. You're trying to find out, "What is your point of view of what I taught today?"** I'd spent too much of the lesson talking about how to share the pieces. That was important feedback that I needed to know as a teacher. She'd missed the big question! And she'd missed it because she'd focused on something that I'd emphasized too much.

Be Flexible

What you do with Afternoon Wrap-Up time should always be based on how children are reacting. Don't plan an agenda—see where the children take you. While it is nice to have a timeline, you always need the flexibility to say, "Could I extend my lesson here?" You need to recognize what children need and then find a way to give them that.

Some days the children are tired, and you're trying to play a game that reviews something and you're getting nowhere. Those days, you're better off sharing a great book with them and ending the day that way. Having options is so important in Afternoon Wrap-Up.

Beginning the End of the Day

We pack up the home-school folders at the end of the day. That's when they get their folder back, and I tell them to pick up their mail and put it in their folders. That's the signal that our day is coming to an end. They know that they need to get organized and packed up because we're going to Afternoon Wrap-Up next. If someone has forgotten her home-school folder, I'll let her borrow one of the "Mrs. Whyte" folders.

Check Your Mailbox

What we *don't* do at the end of the day is pass out papers. We say, "You all know where to find your mail, in the mailbox. Pick up your mail!" "The mail" means any papers that have been corrected, any printed announcements from the office, maybe a book order—any papers or other things that need to go home. All that stuff goes in the mailboxes. You or the student teacher can sort it whenever you want; it doesn't have to take time away from teaching. And if everybody's getting a copy of the same thing, someone just stands at the mailboxes and puts one slip of paper in every slot. Of course, email has allowed us to really cut down on the amount of paper we send home. Messages can be sent to parents at the end of the day, meaning that only the parents without computer access need the printed copy.

> **Save time. Use mailboxes to distribute papers instead of passing them out at the end of the day.**

Sometimes when they lose something, children will come and say, "Well, did you find it?" And I say, "Better look in your mailbox because if I found it, that's where I put it." Mailboxes don't have to be fancy. You can make them by washing out a bunch of old half-gallon milk cartons and stapling them together.

While the children are checking their mailboxes, the student teacher is leaving the home-school folders on the children's desks. Just like the teacher, the student teacher is allowed to ask for help whenever she needs it. Often in the afternoon you'll hear a student teacher say, "Cara or Amanda, can you please put the announcements in the mailboxes while I do the folders?" Or a child will give half the folders to a community helper who helps pass them out.

Everyday Checklists

Don't wait for something to go wrong to create a plan to solve the problem. In your classroom, let's say you always send a book home with each child. How are you going to make sure that book goes home? Are you going to accept the excuse the next day, "I forgot my book"? Or are you going to take preventative measures?

Give the children a way to remember the book. If the book is part of what's supposed to go home every day, then when students get their home-school folder back at the end of the day, one of the first things they should see there is a checklist. And one of the first things they should see on that checklist is the book. Getting children used to that organizational habit, so that they can't use the "I forgot" excuse, is really important.

> **Include a checklist in the home-school folder to help children build habits around being responsible.**

You will find that some children do not need you to help with organization; these children are the ones who have already built trust that they are *responsible*. It is also good to remember that some of our children may still need support to ensure that everything that is supposed to go home—does. In my class, I had some of the children check for the following: Do you have your mail? Do you have your homework? If you're taking home your book, do you have it? Do you have your ABC chart in your folder?

The last line on the everyday checklist was for "A Good Answer."

For what? For when Mom or Dad asked, "What did you do at school today?" I always said, "You won't be able to check that one yet!" And then we'd go to Afternoon Wrap-Up, and part of Afternoon Wrap-Up was devoted to finding a good answer. But I loved it when the children got to where they said, "I'm going to check it now because I already have a good answer!" That's the whole point.

When you get to a point in the year that you begin to see that the children you are supporting are doing a good job, make a list of what to remember, laminate it, and staple it to the same spot where the pad of checklists used to be. Then all a child needs to do is read through the checklist to be sure he has everything.

⭐ **The idea is that the children who need this support can go down through the list and ask, "Do I have this?"—making them more responsible and releasing *you* from having to be such a checker.** We did that unless the child never got it. Sara was a child who had a stack of checklists stapled in her folder, and each day I wanted to see it before she left the classroom. I'd say, "Sara, hon, I want to see actual checkmarks that you did that."

The "I Need" Checklist

Not every class needs this, but you may want to create this checklist so it is ready to go into the home-school folders. It's an "I Need" checklist, and it's mostly for school supplies. We used one of these in my class while we were in a terrible budget crunch. Children were running out of pencils, erasers, and paper. My coteacher and I were spending a fortune on supplies. And the other teachers said to us, "Just make a little checklist. Give your students a copy with the things they need checked

> An "I Need" checklist in the home-school folder can help you collect needed school supplies. Use an "I Need to Remember" note for specific needs that crop up throughout the year.

and have them take it home in their folders." So it actually said, "I need pencils," or "I need paper," or "I need crayons." All those can be on the "I Need" checklist in the folder, and it can quickly be added to the folder.

The "I Need to Remember" Note

The "I Need to Remember" note is for times when there is something the students need to remember to bring to school. These are premade little notes that say, "I need to remember." The children are responsible for filling them in at the end of the day if one is needed. Maybe tomorrow we're going to be doing something outside, and they need to bring mittens; maybe they need to bring back a signature on the field trip slip; perhaps the children need to bring in an egg carton for a project. Anything like that goes on an "I Need to Remember" note. You might create one like this:

> Name _____ Date _____
> I need to remember to bring _____ by _____.
> Please help me remember!

"Oops" Slips

There can be two kinds of "Oops" slips. One is for something the child forgot to bring in. The other is for something the child forgot to do. Each has a space to write what the child forgot. You can add a line for the teacher's signature and a line for the student's signature. We've made a deal in our classroom. The student didn't do what she needed to do, or she didn't bring the field trip slip that she was supposed to remember. She needs to bring it by Thursday. If she came to school the next day and said, "I forgot the slip," that would be Oops #2, and she'd take another "Oops" slip. She'd get one more shot. After Oops #3, I'd call her home. I needed that permission slip because it was important that she go on the field trip.

Use "oops" slips and a three strikes policy to address frequent offenders.

The "Oops" slip is a quick form to use so that you don't have to write lots of little notes. You can just fill out "Oops" slips for things that happen every single day. Then send them home in the folders. Here is a sample:

Name _____ Date _____
Oops! I forgot _____.
Please help me remember it for the next class.

_____   _____
Teacher Signature   Student Signature
Slip # _____

Name _____ Date _____
Oops! I didn't _____.
I need to _____ by _____.

_____   _____
Teacher Signature   Student Signature
Slip # _____

That Amazing Folder

The home-school folder should provide you with lots of opportunities to connect with the children's homes. It also creates teaching opportunities for you and the children who need to learn responsibility and to be a bit more organized. ⭐ **The truth is that you can find lots of "teachable moments" with the folder, even with something as simple as the "I Need to Remember" note.** Maybe sometimes you'll go to Afternoon Wrap-Up with your whiteboard to write on. You'll give each child the "I Need to Remember" slip of paper and you'll say, "There's something you need to remember for tomorrow that's very important." Maybe it's the mittens. "I'm going to write that word (or phrase) up there, and I need you to put it on your 'I Need to Remember' note." That's one more opportunity for them to learn that word and to practice writing it while you're modeling for them. That's an amazing folder.

Self-Evaluations

This could be the time of day for self-evaluation. I am aware that many of you are required to do some type of home-school chart for behavior, and so I have described one that I used here. At the same time, I would like to add a caution to this section. Over the years, I have spent countless hours stamping smiley faces and now I wonder if any of that time was well spent. We expect children to behave, and I don't believe that we need to send a smiley home every day to confirm that the children did what we expected of them. When I go to a store, I don't expect a sticker on my way out and a clerk to say, "Thank you for not stealing today." I am expected to do the right thing, and if I don't, then there may be a note or phone call home. The idea of setting up children to believe that we will report daily on something that we expect just isn't the real world. If we need children to make changes, then they need to self-evaluate. No one is motivated to change something that they don't personally recognize as inappropriate.

The ABCs of My Day

When you come out of college and start to teach, you're led to believe that if there's a behavior problem, you say to the child, "I'll call your parents." So, okay, you call the parents. And of course the parents are in total agreement with you on everything the child has done wrong, and then the child is so contrite that he is just a lovely child who wouldn't ever do anything like that again. Oh, I'm so sorry—I must have been in a dream!

⭐ **I think we need to let children evaluate their own behavior, since they're the ones who can change it.** That was the thought behind The ABCs of My Day. It goes on the right-hand side of the home-school folder. That's the "bring right back" side. The ABCs of My Day was the first thing the children worked on when they got their folders back at the end of the day.

"ABC" is shorthand for "Hey, how was my Attitude today? What about my Behavior? And how did I do as part of the Community?" It's like a behavior log, but it covers more than just behavior. It gives children a chance to learn what we mean by attitude and community. It gives them a chance to practice evaluating their own behavior. And that's a good thing!

> **Have children use the ABCs of My Day as a self-evaluation:**
> **A - Attitude**
> **B - Behavior**
> **C - Community**

On our ABC charts, we used highlighters so that each child could show how he thought he did that day in each of the three areas: attitude, behavior, and community. We used colors just because when we started it in kindergarten, children couldn't write letters or words. So we had a definition for each color.

Your definition may be different from mine. You know what you expect from the children you're teaching in your classroom this year. You may have different expectations next year. So your definitions may be different, and your colors may be different from the ones we used. But the idea is the same for any class.

This is the letter that I sent to parents to explain the chart:

> Dear Parents,
>
> This year priority will be placed on teaching children to identify problems, brainstorm solutions, and evaluate results. One of the most valuable things we can teach children is to assess their attitude, behavior, and teamwork so that they can plan accordingly.
>
> The ABCs of My Day will let us work together to help the children reach this goal.
>
> A is for Attitude
>
> B is for Behavior
>
> C is for Community (teamwork)

Each day, the children will complete their charts according to how they believe they have performed that day. They will use the color coding outlined on the chart. I will be checking the charts daily to determine whether the children's evaluations match my own. At times, the children and I will not agree on a certain evaluation. I may ask a child to reevaluate and make a change, but I will not insist that the child change it for me. Instead, if the student believes he deserved one color and I believe it should be a different color, I will mark the chart with a "DA" (don't agree). If you see that on the front of the chart, you should flip the chart over to view my comments.

We will be completing our charts each day. I ask you to sign your child's chart at the end of each week. If you wish, you may also make comments on the back.

If you have any questions or comments, please feel free to contact me. I look forward to working with you to instill responsibility in the children, and to ensure a happy and safe learning environment.

Yours in learning,

In my class, we started by using a green highlighter to mean "super." Blue for my children meant "good." Yellow was "okay:" you had some rough spots today, but you worked on them. We're going to accept that as okay—as a life lesson—and we're going to move on. Orange was "unacceptable:" you bit someone, slapped someone, swore, or refused to do something. Orange was my highlighter.

Let's say I'm coming around the room while you have your home-school folder out and you're filling out the ABC chart for Monday. And I say, "Ayo, look at that. You gave yourself green for behavior. Green. What does green mean, sweetie?" Get them to say it. *They* have to own it to believe it.

"What does green mean again? That's right: super behavior. Ooh, Ayo. I'm thinking of this afternoon when we came out of the cafeteria, hon, and you tripped Jennifer. Do you remember? Jennifer fell. But you know what? Green is super. That is not super behavior."

And Ayo says, "But I said, 'Sorry'!"

Then I might say that it was okay; it still wasn't super. I might say, "I heard the way you said, 'Sorry.' You remember the two words that go together? You have to say, 'I'm sorry.' You also need to let the person know why you are sorry." ⭐ **So many of our children just say, "Sorry" to get out of something. Teach them the true gift of apologizing.**

Each ABC chart lasts for a month. Parents sign it at the end of each week. At the end of the month, I file each ABC chart in the individual folder I keep for that student. I can use the charts to track the children's progress during the year; observing differences over time makes more sense we when are looking for changes in behavior.

Changing the Chart

If children need to change the chart, they change it just by going over it with the new color. And you can tell what they mean. That's why we made the lightest one yellow. The "okay" was always yellow because I might say, "Well, it was okay, but really, I thought you did a good job about getting back in line. I might give you the blue." Then you might put blue over yellow. You could tell it was blue over yellow; it doesn't mix to green. If it was any lower than yellow, it was my orange pen. Everybody could tell that one because nobody else had orange. I was the only one with the orange pen.

If the children changed the highlighting to yellow, they normally went over it, and if I couldn't tell that it was changed, they'd put a Y at the end of it. If they changed it to green and I couldn't tell, they'd put a G. Some children would say, "I don't think my mom's going to know that that was really 'good.'" "Well, put a *G* next to it."

They really learn pretty quickly what your expectations are. They even learn to justify their assessment. You go by the table and you don't even say anything to them, and they say, "I gave myself 'good' because after it happened . . . ." That's fine. I wasn't going to say anything. They are learning to self-evaluate.

But what if Ayo wasn't going to change her green? She still thought her behavior was super. Was I going to let her take it home and let her parent think she'd been super? No. I bent down and marked it "DA" with my orange pen. "DA" next to the child's highlighting meant "don't agree." The parent would flip the page over and see my writing: "I don't agree with her assessment, but she doesn't believe she should change it."

⭐ **If you're my student, it's okay if you don't want to change the way you marked something. I can't make you change it if you don't believe it because then all I've done is try to control you.** You don't really believe it; you changed it because I told you to. So if you're not going to change it, if you really think that your behavior was excellent, then I want you to leave it. But in my eyes that wasn't super behavior. It's something we need to work on together over the year. And your parents need to know that.

There's another side to looking over what the children have marked, and that's our Alejandro and our Erin—students who don't realize how golden they are. These are the children who get passed over because they demand nothing. No matter what you ask them to do, they try to do it to the best of their abilities. And then I'd get to the end of the day and I'd see Erin giving herself yellow. I'd say, "Erin, honey, what does yellow mean on attitude?" She'd say, "Okay." So I'd write "DA" on her chart as well. And then I'd flip it over and write, "I think Erin had a super attitude today. She did . . .," pointing out to her what she did that made it super.

The Orange Line

The orange pen is the most serious one, and you have to be careful using it. I think sometimes teachers get into this "control" mode. A teacher might not even realize it, but she starts feeling like, "I'm going to control the children in this class." That's when the orange pen becomes the teacher's chance to pick on everything. That's not good.

You can have control without going overboard. I don't want to control how the child feels about it, but there are times when there has to be an orange line on that ABC chart. The orange line is more serious than a "DA." It's more than just "Read my comment about the tripping." It's for something that's totally unacceptable. If there's an orange line, Mom and Dad are going to get a phone call from me or a note home that they need to sign.

> **Have a system to communicate to children and parents when unacceptable behavior has happened. I use an orange line.**

I'll just walk by and mark that orange line on the chart. There's a lot going on at the end of the day, and I don't have time right now to explain again why I feel that your behavior was so serious. We already talked about it when it happened, when you poked James in the eye. But the truth is that I need to talk to your mom and dad about that because James had to leave the room and go to the nurse, and I told you what I'd do: "I'm going to give your mom and dad a call later." I don't have time at the end of the day to go through that again with the child, but I try to mark the orange line on the ABC chart so that everybody knows I'll be in touch with the parents about that behavior.

An orange line doesn't have to be for behavior. A child can get an orange line for attitude or community, too. Maybe I said to Matthew, "I really need you to try to sound that out," and he said, "No!"

I said, "I really need you to work on your morning work."

"No!"

"I need you to join the group."

"No!"

Matthew refused all day long. He wasn't willing to try. That could earn an orange line.

I'd use an orange line for community if a child said, "I didn't read any books today. I'm not cleaning up the book center." It's when a child point-blank refuses to be a part of our class community. That transfers to the playground, too. The way we treat others in our school community is just as important as our classroom community. The orange line is for something that goes beyond a few reminders. It's for something serious enough to "write home about."

Model Appropriateness

When I was working in a district, I observed a teacher, who happened to be using my ABC chart, ask a student if he believed that his behavior that day was *appropriate*. The child rolled his eyes and almost appeared to be contemplating whether to say, "Yes" or "No." Finally he said, "Yes." The teacher raised her voice, "NO, that behavior was NOT *appropriate*!" I believe that this was a case of failing to teach academic vocabulary to a child. I don't believe that the boy knew what the word *appropriate* meant. Many times we use academic language in the classroom that we haven't explicitly taught to the children. Meetings provide great opportunities to build academic vocabulary. Note your grade level vocabulary expectations (as well as the grade level below and above you), and incorporate the language into your classroom conversation. Using this terminology during meetings and ensuring understanding is invaluable.

Also, remember that if you want to change a child's behavior (or attitude or sense of community), you need to do more than just put an

> It is important to develop a common understanding of the language you'll use with children. Incorporate words like *appropriate* into your conversations, and model appropriate behavior so everyone knows what it means.

orange line on the ABC chart. Children aren't willing to change if they don't see anything wrong with what they do now. Often you'll have a child who says, "I don't have a problem with my attitude!!!!!" He doesn't? ⭐ **Children need to see a model of what's appropriate, and they need to see it in a nonthreatening situation.** When a child is talking to you that way, it's not the time to model it because he won't get it. But if you model it and point it out during meetings each day, you can make the point.

"You know, I watched Eric today. What a great attitude he had. You know what I liked about it?" You point out what's good. You can also give children an example of what a bad attitude is, but you have to show them what's bad about it when it's not happening.

I'm big on "no whining." Whining does not solve problems. There's a time at the beginning of the year when I brainstorm with the children a list of our choices when we have problems. And I'll say to them, "Okay, I think I'll add this to the list. One of my choices is, 'I'll just whine about it.' Want to see me whine?" You do it the way they would—but before they do it. And you say, "Now is that going to solve Mrs. Whyte's problem? Does anybody have a better idea today?" You want to have them look at it and start to evaluate it.

Another time, I model how they can handle the problem. They all knew I was always losing my coffee cup. So I'd say, "Uh-oh, Mrs. Whyte's lost her cup again. Now what am I going to do? I know that whining won't help me find my cup. What else could I do? Maybe I could ask a friend whether she's seen my cup. Aaron, have you seen my cup?" You have to show them that there's a better option.

⭐ **Long-term change requires a child to look at what he's doing now and see something wrong in it himself.** Sometimes it's really hard to change a child's behavior because he doesn't see anything wrong with it. A child may think that when you're mad, what you do is hit the person who made you mad. He thinks that fixes it. Getting him to understand that it doesn't, and to be able to say what would have been a more appropriate response, is something we should be modeling.

"You know, you guys have made me mad today. Mrs. Whyte is feeling really angry." Maybe they didn't behave in the cafeteria. We've all had that. We get there and the cafeteria lady says, "Your class was not following directions at all today!" You expect that your children will behave and do what they need to do. So you get them in line and get them back to the classroom. You're mad. You know they know the rules; they don't choose to follow them. You talked to them about it just yesterday.

That's when I say to the children, "I'm mad, but really, I'm disappointed. In fact, I think I'm even a little hurt because you guys know the rules, and you chose not to follow them. In fact, I think you guys need to give me a minute." And I put my hand up to my eyes and I turn away from them. You do that, and they all look so sheepish. We need to model this: What do I do when I'm mad? Do I go around and hit each one of you? That's not an option. That's *not* a choice.

Watch Your Language

With young children, it's all in the language. Never use angry words. Children react so differently to you when you don't sound mad. Don't look mad, either; your manner means a lot. Explain that a child has made a bad choice, and there are consequences for that choice, but do it in a matter-of-fact way. You can express disappointment; just remember you are the model for behavior, and it is important that children see that we have options for how we handle disappointment, frustration, and anger.

> **Replace angry words and facial expressions with matter-of-fact language about choices and consequences.**

I'll use Corey as an example because he was the extreme. He would crawl under the desk. When it was time to start something new, he'd climb under the desk and start kicking and screaming. The bottom line: he didn't like change and he didn't transition well. Then I had two choices. I could say, "Corey, get out from underneath that desk and get in this line!" (That's what people did to me when I was a student.) And I can tell you, 9 out of 10 times, if I got within distance of Corey, he was going to spit at me. Because that's what he did: whenever anyone made him mad, he spit at them. My other choice was that I could keep my face from looking mad and say, "Corey, that's not a good choice, hon."

The fact was that he'd already made his choice. So you need to get over that part and figure out how you're going to get a child who behaves like Corey to make a different one. You do that by putting the decision back in his hands. "You made a bad choice, babe. Right now you have two options. You can get out from underneath the desk yourself and get in line, or you can take my hand and I'll take you over there. But this is not really a choice that's acceptable, so which one do you want?"

I gave him back his power. ⭐ **Ultimately I can't make a child do anything, but I can facilitate his learning to take control and do the right thing.** The minute I started doing that, 9 out of 10 times, he was out from under the desk and in line. Wasn't that what I wanted? There would still be that 1-in-10 time when I had to physically remove him and carry him down the hall while he was spitting at me. I admit it! But 1 time in 10 was better than every time!

⭐ **We tell the children to "use kind words." We need to remember to do the same thing. In the end, no matter what, the whole class is built on deciding whether to make a good choice or a bad one.** I didn't even realize it until someone pointed it out to me, but I use "babe," or "sweetie," or "hon" a lot. It softens the message, so I can say, "That was a bad choice, hon," without sounding mad at the child.

A Report Card for the Teacher

Every day, you ask children to evaluate themselves, and then you review what they say. While you're doing that, every once in a while it's fun to let the children evaluate you. Create a report card for the teacher. Every once in a while we bring it out at Afternoon Wrap-Up, and I say to the children, "I'm going to need your help. You're going to help me to decide what kind of day Mrs. Whyte had today." They know the choices are "always," "most of the time," "some of the time," "never," and "don't know." So I'll ask, "Was I kind today? What does it mean to be kind?" And we go through it. "Did I help you when you needed help?" "Did I make learning fun today?" Use any questions that you think you could benefit from asking your students. Don't forget, the students are helping you—this evaluation is for you.

Once in a second-grade classroom, the children came to me and said, "We did your report card." They had picked up the form from the Afternoon Wrap-Up area. The first line was "is kind." And I got an A plus, so I was feeling good about that. But on "is fair," I'd been demoted to a lowercase "a," and I was wondering what that meant exactly.

On "she listens," I was having a little problem there. I got a B. So that meant that most of the time I listened, but some of the time I wasn't listening to them.

The next line said, "is humorous." They'd asked me what that meant, and I'd said it meant to be funny. I got an A there. They probably did think I was pretty funny because that was the day I'd shown up at school with one black shoe and one navy one.

After that was "expects the best." I liked this one because they wrote an A, and then somebody took the time to trace it. So I thought that was pretty good, and it was important for me to know that.

> Every so often, engage children in an evaluation of your day. They enjoy it, and it will help you remember that they see everything—what you intend to teach and the more subtle messages you may not have meant to communicate.

Then I got to the next line, "is organized." Not only did I get a D, but I got the lowercase "d" that goes with it! That was pretty bad. So I was thinking, "The children see that in me. They notice that often I'm running around saying, 'Has anybody seen my coffee cup? I don't know what I did with that paper! Have you seen that clipboard?'"

⭐ **It reminded me that children see not only what happens, but also how the teacher reacts to what happens. I think of that, and it often reminds me to slow down with the children.**

The next line was "has a clean desk." I got a D minus! But I got an A for "is understanding." Probably the reason I've kept that report card all these years is that they said I was fun. And to me, that's the most important thing I can do in my classroom: make sure they know that learning is fun.

Back to the Meeting

Afternoon Wrap-Up began with the children picking up their mail and packing up their home-school folders. Then we'd go back to our meeting area. ⭐ **I wanted to make sure we ended the day the same way we started it: I wanted to build in that routine, and I wanted to make sure everybody was part of a shared community.** I am going to mention here, as I did in the Morning Meeting section, that it is important to remember each meeting can last different lengths of time, accomplish different things, and address different issues. These meetings are built to address the classroom needs, not just act as a routine.

Sharing

One of the first things you can do when children get to the meeting area is to take a few minutes for sharing. This gives the children a chance to participate by sharing questions, thoughts, and answers. This is not "Show and Tell." Afternoon Wrap-Up is a time when you might pose a question or thought about the day and have partners share. You might choose to end the day with a book, song, or poem. ⭐ **The whole premise of reading in the afternoon is to revisit, not to bring in something brand-new.** We know that rereading old favorites helps to create literate children. So if you like to end the day reading, use this time to create literacy with repeat readings so that children are comfortable with the story or information presented. Remember it is the end of the day, and we do sometimes lose some—or all of them!

A Song

A song can change the pace and get tired children moving. One example is to play an upbeat song that wakes them up a bit at the end of the day. I let them dance while they get mail and pack their folders. Or you can use a song that gets the children thinking. This is a perfect time to play a CD of a song that teaches them about presidents or the alphabet, and then ask the children what information the song shares.

Or you can go in a different direction and use the song that originally went, "This is the way we wash our clothes, wash our clothes, wash our clothes." Just change the lyrics to "Joe (or Jonathan or Nathan) going home to his home, to his home, to his home. Joe is going to his home, and this is what he'll say."

Then Joe needs to come up with an answer to what he'll say if Mom or Dad asks, "What did you do in school today?"

Here's a song/poem I especially like, and children seem to like it, too. It's called "Hop and Skip Workout." It's sung to the tune of "Jingle Bells" (from the *Hop, Skip, Jump to Learn* CD by Donna Whyte and Stephanie Record). Children can recite the words and do the movements at the same time.

Let's all stand up tall
Time to exercise
We'll have fun and laugh
Moving side to side

Let's all sing along
Shake our hands and feet
Listen to the words we sing
Keep moving to the beat

Oh! Skip and Hop, Skip and Hop
Shuffle to and fro
Two steps back and turn around
Jump forward here we go

Oh! Skip and Hop, Skip and Hop
Shuffle to and fro
Two steps back and turn around
Ready here we go

Wiggle your fingers and arms
Give yourself a hug
Heads tucked in and bottoms up
Pretend you are a bug

Stretch your arms and legs
And do a little jive
Slide on over, find a friend
And give a big High Five

Oh! Skip and Hop, Skip and Hop
Shuffle to and fro
Two steps back and turn around
Jump forward here we go

Oh! Skip and Hop, Skip and Hop
Shuffle to and fro
Two steps back and turn around
Ready here we go

Slide over to the right
Tip toe back to your space
Tap your head and touch your nose
March your feet in place

Turn yourself around
Shake your bottom – Oh my!
Stand up straight and flap your arms
Are you ready to fly?

Oh! Skip and Hop, Skip and Hop
Shuffle to and fro
Two steps back and turn around
Jump forward here we go

Oh! Skip and Hop, Skip and Hop
Shuffle to and fro
Two steps back and turn around
Now you're ready to go

The Desk Fairy

One Afternoon Wrap-Up activity could be that we're getting ready for the "Desk Fairy." The Desk Fairy checks everybody's desk at night, after everybody's left, to see what kind of shape it's in. I ask the children, "What's the chance that the Desk Fairy is going to come to my desk tonight?" And I model what she would be looking for.

The Desk Fairy likes clean, organized desks. She doesn't expect us to be perfect. She expects us to be able to find what we need so that we can do a good job. Are the things that you need to get a good start in the morning in a place where we can find them?

They all look at *my* desk and shake their heads.

Well then, chances are the Desk Fairy's not coming to see me.

I let the children think that the Desk Fairy might come any night, so we always need to be prepared for her. I say, "What would the Desk Fairy say is an effort to be organized?" And you know what? I model it and then that night is the night she shows up. What a coincidence!

It's important for the Desk Fairy to notice little things. Some of these children will never have desks that are totally organized—any more than I will! So the Desk Fairy needs to compliment children on whatever is organized. Allow for differences among children, and focus on what they have learned to do, not always what they still can't do.

> **Develop a routine discussion around the Desk Fairy to help children keep their space organized.**

In my school, Sayde was a little girl who had been in my class a few years earlier. Sayde was in seventh grade by this time, and she'd come down and see me after school. So Sayde became the Desk Fairy. It was her idea to have fun with the children. She'd sometimes write a little note to tell a child what he did well or what he should work on. She would sign it "The Desk Fairy." The children were always trying to figure out whose handwriting it was.

A note might say:

> The Desk Fairy was here. She liked that you had your
> pencils sharpened before we even started school today.

And she'd leave a little pile of silver glitter on that child's desk, so that the children would think she'd kind of trailed along there. The Desk Fairy didn't hit everybody's desk, but I'd give her some guidance and make sure she got to certain ones.

When children are young, they love it. By second grade the response is more like, "Who put the glitter on my desk?" But it's still fun. The only thing is, the janitor may not like it. Ours cleaned up a lot of glitter in my classroom.

It helps if you can recruit an older child to be the Desk Fairy, so that the children in your class don't recognize the handwriting on the notes. When Sayde started as Desk Fairy for my classroom, I modeled for her what I wanted her to do. After that, I made sure she left notes for certain children, but otherwise she did it all on her own.

Games and Activities for Review and Assessment

Here's the most important part of Afternoon Wrap-Up: the review. This is when you'll get an assessment from the children in the afternoon to find out where you're going tomorrow. Thinking of years prior to when I started Afternoon Wrap-Up, I always wonder how I knew where the children left me so that I knew where to begin when they came back. I am happy to report that when this can be achieved at the end of the day, you will feel so much more empowered to do what your children need, therefore leading to much higher learning standards.

How are you going to review the day? You're not going to just sit the children down and expect them to tell you what went on today. They're going to be sleeping; they're going to be pinching each other. That's when you need games—for overview, review, and looking forward. I have a few games that I use that you might want to put to work in your classroom. The children think they're fun. I think they're a super way to figure out who got what that day. Here is a list of the games, activities, and assessments that you can choose from each day. Read on for a description of each one.

Mum Ball

Mum Ball grew out of the idea that what was needed at the end of the day was some quiet time—"mum's the word." The only person who's allowed to talk is the person whose turn it is. Otherwise, if you're in my class and you talk when it's

- ☐ Mum Ball
- ☐ Who Wants to Be a Smartie?
- ☐ Secret Ballot
- ☐ Charades
- ☐ That's Bogus!
- ☐ Hey, _____, What Do you Say?
- ☐ Graphic Organizer Wrap-Up
- ☐ What _____ Missed
- ☐ Who Wants to Be the Teacher?
- ☐ Lucky Ducks
- ☐ Guess Crowns
- ☐ Bucket of the Five Senses
- ☐ Who? What? When? Where? Why? How?
- ☐ In My Opinion
- ☐ Magic Recall Spray
- ☐ "Recap" Your Day
- ☐ Beat the Clock

not your turn, you're out of the game. The minute I hear your voice when it's not your turn, you're out of the game.

The children can sit on the floor or stand, and you throw around the Mum Ball. The Mum Ball doesn't have to be an actual ball. I like to use a bean bag toy. I used to use a Nerf football that was shaped like a brain, and I loved it, but the children picked away at it, so I couldn't use that again. The next year I had a mummy doll, which I loved because I'd say, "The mummy is here to play Mum Ball." And the children liked that, but I couldn't find another one when the mummy got filthy. I finally decided the best idea is to find a soft, stuffed critter with appendages because it's so much easier for some children to grab. Many of them can't catch the ball, so that's frustrating when I need them to concentrate on answering the question instead of worrying about their catching skills. If the thing you're throwing has something the children can grab, it's much easier.

As I throw the toy to a child, I ask a question about the day. I might ask that child something specific—something he did this morning that I noticed. I might say, "Nathan, what did you say when you came to my desk this morning? What did you tell Mrs. Whyte? Tell everybody." And maybe we get to repeat that. Or I might ask a question related to a math or science or reading lesson we did that day.

> **Plan to play Mum Ball when you have enough time for everyone to have a turn.**

But how do you keep everybody else involved? Amanda doesn't really care what Nathan told Mrs. Whyte this morning. To keep Amanda involved, sometimes we call "Talk Back" during Mum Ball.

Here's how Talk Back works. I toss the toy to Nathan, and I ask him to tell the class what he said to me that morning. So Nathan says, "Now I know the difference between greater than and less than." He had the right answer, so he gets to choose the next child to get the toy. He tosses it to Amanda.

Then I say, "Okay, Amanda, talk back. This is the only time of the day you can talk back to Mrs. Whyte." "Talk back" means that Amanda is supposed to repeat what Nathan said. The children like Talk Back. It's part of the game.

The other part of the game goes like this. If the child knows the answer to the question, she gets to throw the toy to the next person. If she doesn't know the answer, she throws the toy back to the teacher, and the teacher gets to throw it to the next person. If you know it, you throw it. If you don't, you have to throw it back to me, and I throw it. Either way, *you* get to throw it, and that's important. It's never good to leave someone out. If a student doesn't know the answer, he still gets to throw it, but he doesn't get to decide who to throw it to. So Amanda throws the toy back to me.

> **The Talk Back activity keeps students engaged with what others are saying.**

So then I might say, "Who was listening to what Nathan said?" Somebody will raise a hand. I throw it to that child. He gets to talk back. I say, "You pick. You were on the ball." And then I say, "Boy, Amanda, next time you need to listen, sweetie, because when we play that game, you want to be able to pick."

So the play-by-play goes something like this:

1. I toss the toy to Nathan and ask him a question.
2. He gives the right answer.
3. Nathan tosses the toy to Amanda, and I ask Amanda to "talk back" by repeating what Nathan said.
4. Amanda wasn't listening to Nathan, so she can't answer. She has to toss the toy back to me.
5. I toss the toy to Danny and ask him to talk back.
6. Danny was listening, so he repeats Nathan's answer.
7. Danny gets to toss the toy to Susan.
8. I ask Susan a new question.

At other times I don't use Talk Back. I just start throwing the toy around and asking a question each time it goes out. Once a child has had a turn, he sits on his hands. That way, everyone has an opportunity to participate.

I try to save Mum Ball for a time when I know everyone can have an opportunity. The children get upset if everyone doesn't get a chance.

Who Wants to Be a Smartie?

This started in second grade when the show *Who Wants to Be a Millionaire?* was so popular, and the rules are similar to the show. The children always were enthralled with that program, and they told me they watched it. I thought, "Well, we can play that game. Since I call my children my Smarties, we'll just change the name to Who Wants to be a Smartie?"

When we play Who Wants to Be a Smartie? I divide the class into two teams. I like to tell the partners that one goes to one team and the other to the other team. I ask the first person on Team A a question. Let's say that's Amy. I might say, "Amy, today during Morning Meeting we talked about a different way to write the date. How can you do that?" She might say, "*S-e-p-t.*" I repeat the answer for whoever didn't get it and explain, "That's the abbreviation." I'm hoping it sinks in for the others. It might not; that's the reality. But I'm going to keep at it.

If Amy's answer is right, she gets a point for her team, and the next question goes to the first person on the other team. That's Shamar. If Amy is wrong, or if she doesn't have an answer, Shamar gets a chance to answer the same question and "steal the point." Then Shamar gets a new question to answer, so he has a chance to win another point for Team B. If Shamar doesn't know the answer any more than Amy did, I give the answer and then go back to Amy with a new question.

In this game, you get three lifelines, just like on the TV show—but in this case, it's three lifelines for each *team*, not three per person. The children love using the lifelines. Each team gets to use each lifeline once. Trust me—within the first three children, they've used the lifelines. I always tell them, "You're not going to have any left for the rest of the game." But they don't care; they use them anyway.

Let's say you're a child on one of the teams. One lifeline you can get is a 50-50 from the teacher. If I ask you how the date was written in our Morning Message and you don't know, you can say, "Mrs. Whyte, give me a 50-50." I give you two choices for what you might have seen in Morning Message, and you pick the right one.

The second lifeline is Ask the Audience. In this case, it means you can ask the rest of your team—not the whole class, just your team.

The third lifeline is Phone a Friend. If your class has a phonics phone, that's the time to bring it out because the children love that. I say to them, take your phonics phone and say to the person next to you, "Do you know the answer?" It's that easy.

Sometimes we get other people in the school to play. One time the principal let us call his office. So our Phone a Friend that day was the principal. If you needed the answer, you could call Mr. Spencer. The problem was, for some of the questions I was asking, Mr. Spencer might not have been the best lifeline. If he hadn't been in our classroom, how was he going to know what we talked about in Morning Meeting?

I told the children that, and they still wanted to call him! They called him up and asked, "How was the date written?" And he said, "Was it 'September'?" And they were groaning. And I said, "Guys! How would he know?" It was a life lesson in itself.

Secret Ballot

Secret Ballot is a game I made up one day because I was out of time, and I needed to write a very important note to send home to a parent. The children were saying, "What do we do for review?" And I was thinking, "I'm going to write this note to this parent." So I grabbed the recycling box and dumped everything in it out onto the floor, which they thought was funny to begin with. I threw the box down in the middle of the floor and I said, "That is the ballot box. Every one of you, draw me a picture that shows me something you did today, and throw it into the ballot box."

I wrote the note while the children were drawing. Then I picked out a couple of ballots from the box and I said, "Look at this. What do you guys think this is?"

"That's the butterfly!"

"Ooh, you're right! Somebody says the butterfly came out of its chrysalis today. Did that happen in our class? It's a secret ballot, but that's what somebody says. Who agrees with that?"

They raised their hands. I can still see Andrew, the little guy at the back of the line, shaking his head.

"Andrew, you don't agree with that?"

"No."

"Did you see the butterfly come out today?"

"No."

He'd been in the bathroom. Then he'd gotten called to speech. He'd missed the whole thing. This was my chance to say to myself, "Tomorrow, I need to let him know what went on in our class and at least give him an opportunity to revisit what was an exciting experience for a lot of us."

Secret Ballot was made up the first time. But later on we made it a regular game. First, each child gets a Secret Ballot slip. That means each child gets a ballot with a question or instructions on it. It might say, "What is something we did today?" Or it might ask the child to fill in the blank.

Whatever it says, if your children are young, in the beginning you'll have to read the slips of paper to them; they won't be reading them because most of them can't read yet. So to answer the question, they draw a picture. Later, for my second-grade class, I actually made up little slips that said, "What is something Mrs. Whyte did today? What is something Mrs. Davis did today? What is something Matthew did today?" If Mr. Colburn was our guest that day, it might say, "What is something Mr. Colburn said today?" Some of the children would write, "Hi."

Each child fills out his Secret Ballot and puts it into the box. I don't have time to read or look at all of them. Besides, it's secret! The children don't know who's going to get picked. They just know I'm going to reach into the box and pull out a couple of ballots. And when I pull each one out, they don't know who put that one in.

We made birdhouses one time. Every single ballot that day said we'd made birdhouses. So when I told the children, "Someone said that we made birdhouses," they were all so proud. And when I said, "Who agrees?" every hand went up! Tina said, "Look at the slips of paper! They all say we made birdhouses!"

The idea of Secret Ballot is just getting children to recall something we did that day. It began as a stop-gap activity, but it turned out to be fun, and it got everyone writing for a minute, while I wrote the note that I needed to send home. Then we played off those slips. The children liked it, so that's why I kept it.

Sometimes it's not just the children who learn from the Secret Ballot game. It can be pretty enlightening to look at all the answers after the children have gone home. Let's say one day you read a book you just loved to the class. You read *The Lorax*, and you think the children just loved it, too. Then when you do Secret Ballot, you ask the children what book the class read today. And the answers you get back all say, "We read that l-o-o-o-n-g story!" Then you know you should have spread that book out over several days.

Secret Ballot
What is something _____ did today?

Secret Ballot
What is something _____ said today?

Secret Ballot
Name one thing you know about _____.

The Secret Ballot question is always the same for everybody because we don't want children to know whether it's their answer that I pull out of the box. They might know it's not theirs, but they might not.

Charades

You can act out the review. We do Charades. We started playing Charades with two hearing-impaired girls who were in one of my classes. Those two girls taught me more about teaching children who don't learn auditorially than I ever would have learned otherwise in my whole career.

We started by saying that no one could talk, so you had to get the information across the best way you knew how. I'd give a child a card that might show the name (or a picture) of a character from a story we'd read that day. Or I'd just whisper in her ear to show "The Big Bad Wolf," and she'd have to act that out until someone could guess it.

I think of Amanda. One day her Charade was to show something we'd seen that day. She threw herself on the ground and started rolling around, and I was thinking, "Is she having a fit or is she showing us something?" It turned out that she was showing us how the butterfly had come out of the chrysalis. We were raising monarchs in the classroom during a unit on butterflies. So when Amanda was acting this out, we had to envision the butterfly from the way she was rolling around on the floor and punching out.

Make sure children have opportunities to be silly. It might take time for some of them to come around, but it will be worth it.

It's sad that so many children who are four, five, six, seven, or eight don't feel safe acting or being silly. They're embarrassed. It takes time sometimes to get some of them to come out of their shells. I think it's fun to be silly sometimes. You can review lessons and still give them a chance to be silly and just be children.

That's Bogus

This is a game the children made up. The basic idea is that I'm going to write out several sentences, but only one is true. Students have to figure out which ones are bogus and tell me to erase them. I'm trying to trick them, so they have to be on the ball.

I might give the children these sentences:

We drove to gym.
We ate lobster with melted butter.
We learned to fly.
We used a ruler to measure inches.

It's pretty easy to figure out that *We learned to fly* is bogus. But some of these are harder. I want the children to look for a sentence that sounds as though it could be true, but there's some piece of it that's not true—therefore we didn't do that today. *We drove to gym.* Hey, we went to gym today. What's wrong with that? We didn't drive there. Let partners decide what part makes the sentence untrue. *We ate lobster with melted butter.* We didn't do that. We ate popcorn with melted butter. So that sentence isn't true. Why?

Keep going, figuring out which sentences to erase, until you have just one sentence left. That's the way the children see it—and they're right. But in actuality, you've also reviewed some concepts that you *did* discuss today by saying what you *didn't* do. "We used a ruler to measure inches." That was true. We did do that.

In kindergarten, you might start by giving the children just two sentences, one true and one not. By the time they're in third grade and getting really good at it, you might be all the way up to seven sentences. Narrowing choices is a good skill for children to learn. Children who play That's Bogus now will have an advantage later on, when they need to eliminate some choices on tests before they decide on final answers.

If you have time, you can model writing during That's Bogus, saying the words as you write. Or you can write the sentences on the board before the children get to the meeting area. Or you can say them out loud. Just about anything is fair game, as long as it will get the children interested and participating.

Hey, _____, What Do You Say?

"Hey, Matthew, what do you say? What did you do in school today?" The children sit in a circle. You start the chant: "Hey, Matthew, what do you say? What did you do in school today?" It's a chant, so you have the children clap at the same time. You go right around the circle. They're not allowed to repeat an answer. The first answer will be, "I ate lunch." The second one will be, "I went to gym."

"Okay, guess what, guys? No one else can say 'I ate lunch' or 'I went to gym.' Those are out now. They've already been said."

So you try to get them to talk. The rule is that a child can skip sometimes. She can say, "Skip." At first, sometimes everybody skips. Then it's a pretty short game! If they want to skip, you let them skip. But you really play off the children who *don't* skip. Some children have to learn to speak and to interact with the other children. But once they've learned that, they don't want to skip anymore because they want to feel that they're part of the game.

Usually on any given day, when someone comes up with a good one, I say, "Oh, when my mother calls and asks me, I know what I'm saying today. I'm saying what Annie said. What a great idea!" They want to be the one who comes up with the great idea that the teacher will tell *her* mother.

Graphic Organizer Wrap-Up

Graphic organizers are a great review tool. You can always brainstorm together some ways to fill in a graphic organizer. Just draw a big circle. "Here's today. Tell me some things about today." Or sequence it. "What happened at the beginning of our day? What happened in the middle of the day? What happened at the end?" Teach children to use graphic organizers to lay out the progression of events.

One of the ways I brainstorm with children is to make graphic organizers. I think some of the best ones are just Venn diagrams. Remember the mental "me" folder that each child is bringing to school with him—the one that says, "It's all about me"? We need to build on that thinking and get them thinking about how the things they've learned tie into their own lives.

Maybe you have a Venn diagram that says to each child, "Here's the character; here's you."

"How are you like the character in the book? How are you like the Big Bad Wolf in the story of 'The Three Little Pigs'? And how are you different?" Maybe you can tie it into what they know already and can play off that.

Maybe you've been studying butterflies. Maybe one side of the Venn diagram is "me," and the other side is butterflies. So if you're a student, you should be thinking, "How am I like a butterfly? Ooh, we both grow. I grow, and butterflies grow." So that goes in the center, where the two circles overlap. The next question would be, "How am I different from a butterfly? Well, butterflies fly around. I don't fly; I walk. So I'll put 'fly' on the 'butterflies' side of the diagram, and I'll put 'walk' on the 'me' side."

What _____ Missed

You might say to the children, "Adam wasn't in school today, and we had a long day together. Adam missed some things. So we want to put something in his mailbox that will tell him what he missed. We want to recall some important things we did today that Adam missed, so that I don't forget that, as a good teacher, I need to go back and talk to Adam about these things. So if you remember something that you learned or did today that Adam might need to know about, I'd like you to raise your hand. Let's write it up here. And then we're going to write who said it." It's funny how the children don't want anybody to feel bad that they've missed something.

> Create a graphic organizer by drawing a bunch of little quote bubbles.

Create a graphic organizer by drawing a bunch of little quote bubbles. The children like this bubble organizer because everybody has a chance to be included. I like it a lot because it's a great review tool, and it gives me a way to send home to Adam's parents a list of what we covered. I mark the date on it. That way, if I forget to say something, then at least this went home to his mom, and if she has any questions about it, she can always ask me.

In the beginning, you're lucky if the children fill six of these little quote balloons. But eventually, the list will get bigger and bigger because everyone wants to add her two cents about what went on. When you encourage children to talk, they want to talk. Eventually, I made a sheet that had nothing on it except speech bubbles to tell Adam what he missed. We had 18 bubbles. All those cents added up to big learning! We learned from one another. I'd fill in the speech bubbles as the children came up with ideas. Or sometimes we made this the interactive bulletin board. At the end of the day, I'd say, "Go to the interactive bulletin board and fill in your speech bubble. This might not work for the youngest children, but the older ones like filling in their own bubble.

Who Wants to Be the Teacher?

Maybe the class is working on some kind of graphic organizer. You ask, "Who's willing to be the teacher and show Mrs. Whyte doing something today?" Anyone who's ever been a teacher and watched children play school has said, "I don't sound like that!" They imitate me, and I think it's funny. You should have seen this one child imitating me searching all over my desk for my coffee cup. It was pretty funny!

They're watching us. We need to be careful to remember that they're imitating how we react to things and what we do, what we say about what we do when we can't write, what we do when we can't read something, and what we say when we can't find something. We need to remember that if we let them be the teacher. It can be a humbling experience!

Lucky Ducks

I have two little "duck ponds" that we made out of tin cans. There are sticks in each one. Each stick has a duck sticker at one end and a child's name at the other end. So when I need to pick who goes next, I pick a Lucky Duck. I go to the first pond and grab the duck end of a stick to see whose name is on the other end. Once a child has had her turn, I put her Lucky Duck stick in the other pond. All the ducks swim the same way, so everybody gets a turn. And then they all go back the other way.

> Use an activity like Lucky Ducks to make sure you are calling on every student.

Guess Crowns

For this one, we make crowns out of manila-folder-weight paper, and then I pick a Lucky Duck. I say, "Okay, you get to wear the crown." So if Alannah is the Lucky Duck, I put the crown on her head. The key to the game is that if you're the crown wearer, you don't know what's on the crown. You have to ask questions to figure out what it is. If I'm a kindergarten teacher, maybe the first thing I put on every one of those crowns is one letter of the alphabet. So the children know it's always going to be a letter. When they're older, they can handle a higher level of questions, but I like to keep it pretty simple in the beginning.

The crown wearer can ask another student a question, but the other student can say only, "Yes" or "No." If a student gives a wrong answer, then I have to step in and model for that child how to figure it out.

So the crown wearer might say to another student, "Am I *B*?"
"No."
"Am I *C*? Am I *D*?"
It's probably better to say, "Am I at the beginning of the alphabet? The middle? The end of the alphabet?" You will probably have to coach them to do that.

"Am I between *A* and *E*?"

The crown wearer asks another child yes or no questions until she gets a "No." Then she moves on to the next child.

With an older child, you might tell him that what's on the crown has to do with something he learned in school that day. So that child might ask, "Am I a word?" If he gets a "No," then he might ask the next child, "Am I a picture of something?" Or "Am I a dog?"

I facilitate the questioning by saying, "Guys, remember: Did we see any dogs in our room today? No? What did we do today that might be on that crown?" I'm trying to get them to refocus. Just the idea that they might have a word is so hard for children. They need to learn higher-level thinking skills, to take the clues they're getting, and put them together. One child just said it wasn't a word. So then the child with the crown asked whether it was a picture. And then he said, "So am I the word *have*?"

"Well, wait a minute, you can't be the word *have*. We already established that you're not a word!" Depending on the student's level, sometimes we have to list things on the board. You need to get them to understand that they can play off the progression.

"Am I red?"

"Yes."

"Am I round?"

"Yes."

"Am I an apple?"

You need to keep them working on the progression so that they can develop higher-level thinking skills. This builds children's ability to do riddles, and riddles are a great way to get children thinking out of the box.

If children have difficulty with the idea of asking yes/no questions, then make the questioning more open ended and see what the children can do.

Bucket of the Five Senses

We have a Bucket of the Five Senses, which is a standard beach bucket containing cards with pictures of hands, ears, mouths, noses, and eyes on them. A child gets the bucket and has to pick one of the cards. If she draws a card with ears on it, I ask, "What did your ears hear today?" The child might answer, "I heard Mrs. Whyte read a book." If I want to get her talking more, then the bonus question would be, "What was the book?" I don't always use a bonus question, but often I want more. I want to know what the story was about or who one of the characters was.

Who? What? When? Where? Why? How?

The ability to ask and answer questions is a critical skill and a key element in today's ELA standards. This is also another fun way to review the day during Afternoon Wrap-Up. Start with one slip of paper for each child in the class. On each slip of paper, write either "Who," "What," "When," "Where," "Why," or "How." Put all the slips in a container, and have a child draw one. Then the child has to ask a question about something discussed in class that day that starts with the word on the slip of paper he's drawn. If a child pulls out *Why*, for example, he might say, "In *Sarah Plain and Tall*, why did Caleb keep asking Anna about their mother?" If the word is *Who*, he might say, "Who is telling the story?" Or if he draws *When*, he might say, "When did Sarah join the family?" You're teaching children to formulate questions for other people to answer.

In My Opinion

Place a statement on the chart that pertains to something from your day. Ask children to respond, "In my opinion, ..." For example, you could write, *"My favorite activity today was working on the pumpkin research project."* Children share their opinion of the statement with a partner. They also have to explain why they feel that way. This is a terrific lead-in to having children write opinion texts—another of the new ELA standards.

Magic Recall Spray

Over the years, it has dawned on me that I can get children to participate in pretty much anything I want them to by simply adding a "gimmick" to it. The magic recall spray activity involves my dollar store purchase of a plastic spray bottle, filled with colored water and a tiny amount of glitter. I shake it up and tell my students that if they are having a hard time remembering something we did today, I will spray them with the magic recall spray. Most kids love it, but of course I would never spray a student who didn't ask me to or whose parents objected!

> **Use a gimmick to engage children in the activity—it can be very powerful.**

"Recap" Your Day

I have created special visors that the students wear when they are "recapping" their day to their partner. They are the plastic visors that come several to a pack from a dollar store and are then decorated with stickers and pom-poms. After the first child has had a turn, I tell partners to switch. This is a great visual for showing which partner is supposed to be the talker and which is the listener.

Beat the Clock

I don't want for one minute to fool you into thinking that every day everything will be so hunky-dory that time doesn't get away from you. It does. ⭐ **But how you choose to beat the clock makes the difference.** You've got to beat the clock. You're running out of time. How can you do it in a fun, lighthearted way that doesn't put children under that stress of, "Get the heck out the door!"?

I think you can do it. Set a timer and tell the students, "We have to really pick up our feet. Do you know what it means to have fast feet?" That's a little different from, "GET GOING!" It makes a huge difference how you choose to end the day and the words you choose to use.

Yes, there are going to be times, so be prepared. Don't wait for those times to happen. Know what your strategy is going to be. Are you going to say, "Leave the books; we don't have time to get them"? There *is* going to be a time when you realize, "Okay, I'm out of time. If I try to shove this all in, I'm going to stress out these children, and I'm going to stress myself. The mittens are going to be here; the lunch boxes are going to be here. What's the most important thing I need to do to get them out the door in the next 30 seconds? I need their lunch boxes in their hands and their mittens on them."

So: "Everybody make sure you have your lunch boxes and your mittens, and we're going to need to get going. Don't worry about the rest of it today. We'll worry about it tomorrow." Figure out ahead of time how you're going to handle this.

Have you ever played that game Beat the Clock? It used a little clock, and that's what I used. It actually was a loud little clock. The children heard that, and they knew it was counting down, and they'd laugh about it. We did it in a lighthearted way, but the reality is that children need to get out the door. It's just a question of how you do it. We used that little clock, and when that gave out we used a little one-minute timer that ticked loudly. We want children to hear the ticking the same way we're hearing it.

Learning on the Way out the Door

The Closing

We want to say good-bye. We want to see the children out the door or out at the bus the way we saw them when they came in. One way to do that is to play a game that gets the children to the door. I liked to recite a rhyme that went like this:

One, two. I'll give a clue: It's red (or blue or yellow).

Three, four. When you're at the door. (So they have to get to the door in order to play.)

Five, six. Who will I pick? (You have to be at the door for me to pick you to figure out my clue.)

Seven, eight. I cannot wait. (So if you're not at the door, I'm not going to pick you.)

Nine, ten. Show me when. (Use our special signal to show me when you're in line and ready with the answer.)

As soon as the children are where they need to be, have them give a signal that shows they're ready. You can have them give a thumbs-up or close their eyes. Or ask them what they'd like the signal to be. They'll come up with some good ones!

Learning Line-Up

When it's time to line up, the children tend to get pretty hyper, so this is a good time to sing a little song or do a little chant. You might sing a song that's on my CD, *Sing Yourself Smart*. The tune is "Twinkle, Twinkle, Little Star," but I changed the lyrics. Try something like this:

> *Mrs. Whyte's hourglass.*
> *Time to clean up in our class.*
> *Hurry, hurry, don't delay.*
> *Time to put your things away.*

You can play line-up games, too. Maybe you ran out of time today. You didn't have time to review. So play a learning game. Have the children line up by height, or by the color of their shoes or shirts. Or pick a color and say that anyone wearing that color gets to be first in line. You say, "Anyone who has red on gets to be first." And they're looking at one another and saying, "You have red on!" You're getting them to play games at the same time you're trying to get them to do something organizational. You can use a poem or make up a song. The rule is that by the time I get to the end of the song, they need to be in line.

> *Good-bye, good-bye, my Smarties,*
> *Time to go . . . Line up, please!*
> *Check for notes, books, and backpacks,*
> *Won't be long till we'll be back.*
> *Good-bye, good-bye, my Smarties,*
> *Time to go . . . Line up, please!*

(To the tune of "Where Is Thumbkin?")

> *Off to your house, off to your house,*
> *Our day's done, our day's done.*
> *We'll be back together, we'll be back together.*
> *Tomorrow, tomorrow.*

Saying Good-bye

When the children are lined up at the end of Afternoon Wrap-Up, they need to turn and say good-bye. They can shake hands, or they can wave. Sometimes I ask each child to shake the hand of the person behind her and the person in front of her. If they don't want to shake hands, they can do one of the other Three Hs again; they can give a high five or a hand wave.

You are all familiar with the rhyme, "See you later, alligator." Here are a few versions from *The First 30 Days* Activity CD by Donna Whyte.

> *Out the door, growling boar*
> *Time to scoot, slimy newt*
> *Don't meander, salamander*
> *Give a hug, ladybug!*

You can have your children make up rhymes that they think are a good way to say "good-bye."

In Conclusion . . .

From the moment they walk in the door until the moment they leave at the end of the day, children deserve to be in a place where they feel connected, where the message, loud and clear, is YOU belong here. The routines of Morning Meeting and Afternoon Wrap-Up provide us with daily opportunities to direct the focus to the children during two of the most important times of the day. Throughout this book, I've offered many of my ideas about how to best utilize these times; I know that you will think of so many more. Remember, the most effective routines are flexible, so be sure to make use of those "teachable moments," as they often offer the most direct path from learning to your students. I promise that incorporating Morning Meeting and Afternoon Wrap-Up to your day will add to your class-room in a way that will make you ask, "Why did I wait so long to do this?" Happy teaching!

Index

SDE Professional Development

Who Is SDE?

Staff Development for Educators is America's leading provider of professional development for PreK through Grade 12 educators. We believe educators have the most important job in the world. That's why we're dedicated to empowering educators with sustained PD that is not only research-based, innovative, and rigorous, but also practical, motivating, and fun.

We offer:

- Expertise in the most relevant **cutting-edge topics** and global trends facing educators today

- Access to over 300 engaging and **inspiring educational experts**

- A **variety of PD options** to fit how you learn best and that match your budget and schedule.

Educators need flexibility and variety in accessing professional development.

That's why SDE provides multiple formats to fit how you learn best.

PD Events

- Seminars
- Conferences
- The Academy
- In-Depth Institutes
- Train-the-Trainer Institutes

PD Resources

- Books
- Games & Apps
- Manipulatives
- Digital Resources

Onsite PD

- Customized Conferences
- Hosted Events
- Job-Embedded Coaching
- Modeling/Observation

Web-Based PD

- Webinars
- Online Courses
- Flipped Workshops
- Blended Learning

Contact our Educational Partnerships team for more information or to request a complimentary consultation.

ProfessionalDevelopment@SDE.com
1-877-388-2054 • www.SDE.com

Expect **Extra-**ordinary

Together let's create **extraordinary** classrooms.

SDE **Staff Development for EDUCATORS**

Serving the professional development needs of extraordinary educators

1-877-388-2054 | www.SDE.co